ROCKING WALL ST.

ROCKING WALL ST.

FOUR POWERFUL STRATEGIES THAT WILL SHAKE UP THE WAY YOU INVEST, BUILD YOUR WEALTH, AND

GIVE YOU YOUR LIFE BACK

GARY MARKS

FOREWORD BY JOHN MAULDIN

BICENTENNIAL
1807
☉WILEY
2007
BICENTENNIAL

John Wiley & Sons, Inc.

Published by John Wiley & Sons, Inc., Hoboken, New Jersey.
Published simultaneously in Canada.

Wiley Bicentennial Logo: Richard J. Pacifico

For general information on our other products and services or for technical
 support, please contact our Customer Care Department within the United States
at (800) 762-2974, outside the United States at (317) 572-3993 or fax (317) 572-4002.

Wiley also publishes its books in a variety of electronic formats. Some content that
appears in print may not be available in electronic books. For more information about
Wiley products, visit our web site at www.wiley.com.

Library of Congress Cataloging-in-Publication Data:

Marks, Gary.
    Rocking Wall Street : four powerful strategies that will shake up
  the way you invest, build your wealth, and give you your life back /
  Gary Marks.
      p.   cm.
    Includes bibliographical references.
    ISBN 978-0-470-12487-1 (cloth)
    1. Hedging (Finance).   2. Investments.   I. Title.
    HG6024.A3M353   2007
    332.64'524—dc22   2006034738

Printed in the United States of America.

10 9 8 7 6 5 4 3 2 1

To:

Hedge fund manager, Mike Masters.

*Stephen Pollan, financial planner
and author of the best-selling book,* Die Broke.

Bob Dylan, who in the 1960s helped me to think beyond many lies.

*John Lennon and Paul McCartney, who first taught me about joy,
and the life I wanted to lead.*

Contents

Part Two: Knowing the Difference between Market Stats and Market Hype

Part Three: Hedging Wall Street: Hedged Portfolio Construction

Part Four: Planning for the Future and Seeking the End Game

Foreword

I've been very fortunate in my professional life. I've traveled around the world and have been able to meet some of the most intelligent and provocative people in the investing arena and other fields. Listening to and in many instances working with these great minds has helped me develop and grow. Occasionally, I feel as if I'm spending too much of my time away from my home and covering too many cities in too few days. Fortunately, my children—or their concerts, ballgames, and return trips home from schools—remind me of what really matters.

That's why I'm especially pleased to introduce you to *Rocking Wall Street* by Gary Marks. In the first of what I hope will be an ongoing series of books by people I think have a valuable message, this work offers a unique perspective on the investing game and why too many people play it wrong and end up in financially precarious positions instead of more secure ones.

Gary is a professional money manager. He manages money for other people, especially very affluent individuals. He doesn't spend his time flying around the world, meeting clients or fund managers. In fact, he hardly travels at all. Gary prefers to stay close to home—Maui—with his wife and three children. Hey, if I lived in Maui, I'm not sure I would ever want to leave either! In fact, a number of years ago, Gary made a conscious decision to change his life. He was living in California and working at warp speed in the investing profession. He was making lots of money for himself and his clients, but he wasn't particularly happy. With a very supportive wife, he moved to the beautiful state of Hawaii.

There's more to Gary's story. He has another profession as well. He spent a number of years touring as a rock/jazz musician. He has recorded 10 albums since the early 1970s, has taught piano, and has written books on piano technique. In *Rocking Wall Street*, Gary talks about his own life and why he feels that the creative skills he has used in his music help him in his investing strategy. He also explains why he often gives his clients advice that they may not want to hear. Usually, investors want an adviser to tell them how much *more* money they can make. Gary won't do that because he views investing as inextricably tied to risk, as well as to other aspects of life. He will tell his clients to put aside money and invest in a secure, low-risk vehicle, rather than trying to hit a grand slam. Why? The market is simply too unpredictable and Gary has seen people lose their businesses, homes, and sometimes their health and their families. He's baffled by clients who make the same mistakes as gamblers, always assuming that they can beat the house and will manage to outsmart the other players, including adept professionals on the other side of the trade. Unfortunately, gambling and investing are very similar, and that's why Gary's unique view deserves to be presented.

Gary questions many individuals and institutions that are part of my daily routine—financial journalists, investment advisers, mutual funds, brokers, and hedge funds. He's skeptical of the promises, the predictions, and the so-called guarantees that can lull individual investors into making decisions that aren't right for their particular circumstances. He cautions readers to question everything they hear. There are no guarantees in life, and not even the most educated or most astute investment professional is perfect. Of course, you want to work with a financial professional whom you trust and who you believe has your best interests in mind—whether you have $100,000 to invest or $10,000,000 to invest. But, you always have to be skeptical and do your own research as to their motivations.

Rocking Wall Street offers a fresh perspective for investors. It focuses on how to invest, what to invest in, and how to profit with less risk, and gives away a lot of Gary's hard-won knowledge about the investing game. But the book also shows that you can make choices about how much time to you spend investing and worrying about your money, where to live, how long to work, what type of job to have, what kind of lifestyle to enjoy, and whatever other values matter to you. That's one of the key messages of this book. There's nothing wrong with wanting to accumulate wealth or with making lots and lots of money; however, your investing strategy shouldn't simply focus on the money itself—but on what it allows you to do with the rest of your life.

John Mauldin
November 2006

Preface

Safe and *successful* are two words that should never be separated when considering how to invest your money. You will be able to understand how to make successful as well as safe choices by following these four key investing strategies:

1. **The Emotional Controls**
   How to hedge your emotions as well as your investments.

2. **Knowing the Difference between Market Stats and Market Hype**
   There are market statistics, and then there are statistics that are neatly packaged to market you.
   Being able to tell the difference between the two is a key element to successful investing.

3. **Hedging Wall Street: Hedged Portfolio Construction**
   How and why we should make hedging techniques the rule, not the exception, in our investment portfolios.

4. **Planning for the Future and Seeking the End Game**
   See your portfolio of assets, your career, and your personal life as one inseparable investment.

Rocking Wall Street is my attempt to:

☞ Help you find the kinds of risk-averse profits that most investors think happen only in fairytales.

☞ Help you gain peace and freedom inside the investing process so that you can learn to leave this place of investing often and live a happy life back on the outside—because spending too much time thinking about your money *is a terrible waste of the money*.

☞ *Rock Wall Street to the core* so that the hype that is so often perpetrated upon the average investor does not ruin the lives of investors like you in the future.

Acknowledgments

Thanks to:

John Mauldin, of Millennium Wave Investing, author of the best-selling books *Bull's Eye Investing* and *Just One Thing*.

My financial partner, Geoff Gotsch.

My investing teams.

My clients, friends, and partners, from whom I have learned so much.

Denzyl Feigelson, who first suggested I write this book.

Dean and Cheryl Radetsky for their unwavering support.

Amma (The Hugging Saint) for the simple truth.

Special thanks to my wonderful wife, Theresa, and the three *very best* kids in the world.

Advertising signs that con you
Into thinking you're the one
That can do what's never been done
That can win what's never been won
Meantime life outside goes on
All around you.
> —"It's All Right Ma,
> I'm Only Bleeding,"
> by Bob Dylan,
> from *Highway 61 Revisited**

Playing with the stock market is like playing
chicken with a freight train . . . no matter
how many times you win, you only get to
lose once.
> —Mike Masters,
> hedge fund manager

ROCKING WALL ST.

Part One
THE EMOTIONAL CONTROLS

1

The Beginning, and the End Game

Although this book is filled with investing and financial advice for readers of virtually all economic backgrounds and circumstances, it specifically addresses the concerns and questions of those who are, or who aspire to be, *high net worth* investors (legally defined as those with a net worth of $1.5 million or more).

We are going to explore four strategies that could change the way you approach your investment process forever—both before and after you qualify as a high net worth investor.

I will give you specific tools for immediate success that can work under all kinds of market conditions. But we are also going to explore key issues not directly related to the investing of the money itself.

For instance, after you are making a lot of money and are by all normal social definitions considered successful—**how do you get your life back?**

I have met investors in their sixties who have hundreds of millions of dollars and no heirs, who oversee their investments 8 to 12 hours a day, 5 to 6 days a week.

I asked one such individual, "Why don't you just drop everything and go off to Paris for a week?" He responded, "I was in Paris
just last month meeting with two of my managers."

What I really wanted to say was: "When does the money wheel
stop and life begin?"

If you are an active investor—someone who pays attention to
your investments more than once a week (and you're not a licensed
professional)—you may be heading down the same road—where
accumulating money becomes the main goal, all failures are toxic to
your ego, and your life has been kidnapped by the game.

The question then is: How do you strike a balance between
finding time for your family, your friends, and your inner life, while
also making savvy and safe investment and business choices?

Creating free time is of incalculable value. All successful high-
level executives (defined as those who can hire staff at will) must
learn how to delegate a high percentage of their work responsibilities until they reach a level of free time that allows them to think
and dream, rather than just respond to daily crises as they arise. Investors need similar amounts of free time away from the trading
and research to assess the big picture.

When this free time is available, you may also come to ask
questions that are not just investing or business-related, such as
what is the meaning of all this work and free time?

Reading this book—and putting into practice the specific
strategies I discuss—will give you investing tools to last a lifetime. It
will also greatly decrease the time you have to spend worrying
about your investments or about every sharp turn in the market.

We will talk about:

**How to profit *and* protect your assets from serious
losses at the same time.**

**How to steer clear of market hype and avoid the big
mistakes.**

How to plan for your future.

What it truly means to be rich.

If you have ever felt overwhelmed or downright emotionally kidnapped by the investing game, I will also attempt to *give you your life back!* In fact, since I value your time as a reader, let's settle for nothing less.

These first two chapters will have a distinctly personal spin to them—the real story, "About the Author," to help set an emotional backdrop to the more technical discussions to follow.

INSIDE THE BOX WON'T GET YOU THERE

I am often asked, how did a professional rock songwriter living in Maui become a big-time player in the hedge fund business?

Fifteen years ago I was playing concerts with my band in San Francisco, had a publishing deal with Famous Music/Paramount, was finishing my seventh recording of original music, and was teaching the Gary Marks Piano Method—"Learn chords, scales, and how to play songs without reading notation. . . ."

To this day I don't own a suit; I would never wear a tie. I go to the beach most days with my surfer and kayaking friends, while also researching hedge fund managers, co-guiding the investment portfolios of a number of funds of funds, and keeping my investment teams happy, organized, and motivated.

You may think being a rock songwriter, a self-proclaimed beach bum, and the portfolio manager of more than a handful of funds of funds is an odd mix. And admittedly it is. But I also found that these separate worlds could actually create a synergy.

What happened to me at first was relatively simple: When I had made enough money in the music world to consider the idea of investing, I realized very quickly that I wouldn't be able to handle the volatility and uncertainty that average investors typically endure. I read about the history of stock markets throughout the twentieth century, I studied the concept of diversified portfolios, and became even more ill at ease with the traditional investing process as defined by the marketing campaigns that most brokers and advisers use.

My continuing investigation eventually pushed me into considering the world of hedge funds.

I asked a friend who was invested in hedge funds exactly how he would define one. He said, "A hedge fund is either a really stupid or a really brilliant person who has started a limited partnership, and has found either a really stupid or a really brilliant strategy to invest other people's money in. You just have to figure out who the really brilliant ones with the really brilliant strategies are, and avoid the stupid ones with the stupid strategies. And *poof*, you're rich!"

After many years of research, I began to get an inkling of how to tell the difference between stupid and brilliant (and occasionally fraudulent) managers, but the process was considerably longer and more complex than my friend had let on. In fact, just initializing an investment in a single hedge fund now takes a team of due diligence experts a number of months, including gathering background checks on the major principals, and a lot more.

Meanwhile, the lure of the 1990s stock market also led me to day trading. I had some victories, some defeats. Overall I was making a lot of money. But in the end, I felt like life was passing me by, my musical life was fading away, my family was being ignored, and even the big financial victories weren't fulfilling after a while.

This is the odd thing about the investing game (and gambling): If you play it all the time, when you win, it's a pretty good feeling. And you look ahead excitedly to the next challenge or the next bet. When you lose, it's a horrible feeling. You feel like a fool, a sucker, a failure. If the losses are big you want to hide away or run away. You can't enjoy your family or look them in the eyes.

This is not what I call a good emotional trade-off.

Sometime after I stopped day trading I started my own alternative asset management company with $4 million under management. (My friends had been seeking financial advice from me for years since I seemed to have some kind of a knack for it. I passed the Series 7 exam and began a fund of hedge funds.) I decided to hedge our risks every way I could and not aim for the moon. After you've been studying the investing game for a while, you learn that the moon is a moving target, and unless you're an astronaut with a very good team back in Houston, the odds are very low that you will ever hit it, except by accident.

In the first seven years, the company grew to over $250 million of assets under management. To this day I run the company from home on my laptop computer. I have never had an office outside the house. That's because I like working with my kids running around the room, sitting on my lap, and playing my guitars while I'm on the phone. . . . You get the picture. I enjoy creative chaos. Another advantage I had: My family does not watch television. We're not connected to the world of cable. So I had the advantage of *not* watching CNBC and all the other financial media shows. All the while I was writing more songs, making more CDs . . . and having more kids.

A few years ago, a potential investor called me and said he was considering investing $10 million with my firm and wanted me to come to New York to meet him. It was a lot of money and I was quite excited. But I told him I was living in Maui and not interested in flying to New York for a business meeting. He offered to pay the plane fare, but I simply repeated, "I'm in Maui. Why would I come to New York?"

I offered to fly him to Maui instead, but I told him to dress very casually—shorts and a T-shirt would suffice. We then started talking about Maui and how beautiful the beaches were. He told me New York was a grind. He didn't really want to be there anymore. I told him he could afford to live anywhere, but he said his business was there and he couldn't leave. I wondered why he wouldn't just move his business to where he wanted to live. After all, he was personally worth tens of millions of dollars. He could afford to do that for himself. But I left that question for another day. We kept talking about personal things. We discovered we each had a young son, and agreed that fatherhood was the most amazing thing that had ever happened to either of us. I also told him about my music.

After the call he went to my web site and listened to my songs.

A month later he decided to invest without meeting me in person. He gained the final level of comfort he needed without me having to travel to New York. He told me, "It's odd but true that if you had actually been willing to fly six thousand miles just to meet me, and had shown up with a briefcase and a black suit and told me you had a degree in economics from Harvard, I would have been far more skeptical and more on guard about you and your abilities than I am now."

He added, "Economists rarely know how to make money, anyway. You don't learn that kind of thing from books; you learn it from street smarts."

This is a great paradox, and one that is often true about investing, art, or the best-laid retirement plans of financial advisers: The more "inside the box" things are, the more probable it is that the idea will fail.

The specific financial advice I offer in this book is admittedly outside the box. But ask yourself where the typical investing process offered by brokers and financial advisers gets you when you have to make it through bear market cycles like the one that started in the beginning of the twenty-first century? Their ideas and retirement plans were so 1990s.

The 1990s, specifically 1995–1999, were a fabulous aberration. Those who saw this period as a once-in-a-lifetime gift from the market gods kept their profits. Those who thought they learned about investing from experiencing that single decade were set up to be tarred and feathered soon thereafter, and ended up losing vast sums of money in just a few short, painful years. And of course volatile bear markets in all asset classes—real estate, equities, bonds, gold, oil—are just a natural part of the investing landscape.

How can we prevent truly devastating losses from happening to us next time, or the time after that? How can we prevent ourselves from being misled by our market instincts, market gurus on TV, carefully preened market statistics, newsletters, or well-meaning advisers?

The following chapters will attempt to free you from many of the deadly illusions presented as fact by traditional brokers, financial advisors, and so-called market experts, so that you can profit with far less risk than you may have previously considered possible.

THE CRAFT VERSUS THE ART

I started learning guitar at the age of 16. Within a few years I found myself singing my songs in front of, at times, some very large crowds. In my early twenties I was approached by a well-known music manager. He was the manager of a number of jazz greats, and was considering branching out into pop and rock, which was where I fit into his picture.

One day I played him a new song I had written. He looked at me for a while, nodding his head, and then said: "You're a very good songwriter. But if you are going to be successful in this business you have to learn the craft as well as the art. You'll need to become a great craftsman. Or we'll both fail."

I asked him the difference between artist and craftsman. He said: "An artist is an idea person, a visionary. They create something from nothing. A craftsman makes those things accessible to the world, and understands how to detail out the dream. So, for instance, you write great songs and lyrics out of thin air. But a craftsman knows how to pick the right microphone to use in the studio, how to rehearse a band, how to read a contract with his attorney, and how to make good use of the mixing gear in the studio. If he's a lyricist he'll read a thousand books to study the crafts of prose and poetry. A musician-craftsman has a vision of what direction his career is going, beyond just aiming for 'success.' Success in this business sometimes only means you are controlled by the ones who control the money. The craft of this business is to understand how *you* stay in control, rather than just becoming a glorified vacuum cleaner salesman, traveling around from town to town, working for the firm."

I relay this to you now because investing, business, and personal finance each have the same divisions between art and craft.

You may be a visionary inventor and create something never seen before, but not know how to run a business.

You may be a brilliant entrepreneur, but not be skilled at investing. In fact, this is typically the case.

Or, you may be an investor with good instincts about the art of investing, but you do not have enough institutional support or inside knowledge about how the game really works to make those instincts pay off.

The craft inside the investing game consists of various skills, such as knowing the difference between truly relevant market research and media noise or marketing hype; developing a sophisticated level of due diligence; and devising a systematic investing approach that bypasses typical emotional responses.

Only when you begin to master these crafts can you allow the more artful dimensions such as instinct to help guide you.

Without the craft we can't *afford* our instincts. They will cost us too much money. We may end up defrauded, addicted, losing sleep, and losing a fortune, just trying to manage our money by using amateur skill sets in a highly professional and dangerous game of chicken.

In the realm of personal finance, the craft can help you to accumulate wealth safely, create a reasonable retirement plan, and so forth. But the art then allows you to consider how to merge that wealth into a happy, healthy life, day to day. The balance between art and craft will always be critical.

It takes discipline and attention to inner details to bring alive the full vision of the life you seek.

Money can create copious blessings and allow you the free time to do what you truly desire to do, or money can kidnap you away from everything you truly hold dear. To some, money actually becomes more of a burden than a benefit.

What usually is the first thing to undermine us is the gambling aspect of the human psyche—risking everything to go after a pawn while exposing our king. In the following chapters I will show you how to avoid many of the pitfalls and burdens of investing and money, so that you can grow your wealth safely, and at the same time create for yourself a truly rich life.

Let's move on now to one of the main concepts of *Rocking Wall Street*.

THE END GAME

What is the game we're playing? And how do we win?

When individuals are *safely invested*—when they and their families no longer have to be concerned about money—I call this the End Game.

Of course, getting to that point is seen as a rare event in this world. But actually, I believe the End Game can occur for more people far sooner along the money timeline than is commonly believed.

The first thing to realize is that as enjoyable as it may be for some of us to reach this level of success, at a certain point life usually demands more of us.

In 1998, I was "managing" my own money. (The quotation marks around the word "managing" are there because when you manage something in an amateur way, it's not really managing.)

I would be down in my office/music studio (which used to be my music studio/office) buying and selling stocks and mutual funds each day on my laptop computer. One day I came upstairs to find my wife making dinner, with our two-year-old daughter sitting on the countertop watching her every move. They both smiled at me as I entered the room looking haggard and rather nervous. I had had "a very big day" as the title character in the movie *Jerry Maguire* once said.

I hugged Theresa and let out a huge sigh and said, "We made a lot of money today."

She looked at me with her eyes turning just a tad watery (not from the onions, I think) and said, "I'm glad you're taking care of the finances and the investing for the family. But every day you come upstairs nervously happy, or nervously upset, and you tell me what happened as if you've been in a war. Gary, I know you want to be a hero and a great provider for our family. And I love you for that. But to tell you the truth, I'd rather have an 80-year-old Gary with $8,000 in the bank than a Gary who makes $8,000,000 in the stock market and then dies in eight years from a heart attack."

I was truly shaken by this revelation. It was like being awakened from a long dream. What was I doing with my days? When was the last time I had been truly free of stress? Even on weekends I was planning strategy, secretly waiting for the weekend to fly by so I could go back to the game.

I was spending my hours with my mind entangled in front of a computer screen, buying and selling a bunch of names and numbers. I was riveted to the computer, glancing every few minutes at some statistic on CNBC, nervously trying to beat a system that was ingeniously designed to beat the likes of me hour by hour!

Somehow I *was* winning back then and making big money! I had systematically discovered a trading inequity called international arbitrage. I was also playing the speculative dot-com bubble by day trading America Online (AOL), Yahoo!, and Amazon. I was buying them on days when the overall market was trending up, then selling them on the next down day. It was a big rush for me when I won.

But regardless of how I did on a given day, my mind could not let go of the game. The game, as Jerry Maguire's wife once said, "had me at 'Hello!'"

In fact, the game was now playing me, rather than vice versa. It was eating me alive even as I was raising my hands in victory.

I decided to stop day trading immediately. I felt like I had been winning a NASCAR race asleep at the wheel and had suddenly awakened and slammed on the brakes right at the finish line.

I took all of our family money and put it into hedge funds and checked in a few times a month. (But that's *not* something I recommend the uninitiated attempt to do on their own. I will discuss this more in detail throughout the book.) Trust me, if I ever in my life got truly lucky, it was then. Looking back I am amazed that the hedge funds I chose with virtually no due diligence were not extremely risky, or even downright frauds. They did extremely well in both good market months and bad. Not only were the managers great people, but they tutored me in the art and craft of hedge fund investing. They led me to my present career—when I could have instead been led straight off a cliff.

But back to my present point:

If we become more aware of what money is doing to us day to day, then we will naturally become better, more patient, less risky investors over time. We won't allow the game to take us over. When the game takes us over we rarely stand a chance.

When we are in control of the game, we become more effective investors and more effective business leaders. We find that big ideas and ways to implement them come to us more often. This happens because the mind is not overwhelmed with the stresses and minor victories and losses that usually occur each day.

The investment gods hand out appropriate rewards and punishments. Who do they reward? Investors who do the right thing.

What is the right thing?

Following conservative, well-thought-out investment principles is the right thing.

Making sure that we do not allow success and money to run, or ruin, our lives, is the right thing.

The Goal of the End Game

The goal of the End Game is to accumulate enough wealth for you and your family to *stop*.

Stop putting your wealth at risk. Stop the gambling and risk-taking with investments of any kind.

You would finally have enough money and personal power to walk away from the investing game and spend the rest of your life *doing something else!*

When exactly do you reach the end game?

A simple equation can define it:

When you have enough principal invested safely for your after-tax income to match or exceed your annual expenses on an ongoing basis. This would include budgeting for the lifestyle you truly want.

Here is the story of my friend Tim, who reached the End Game and knew what to do about it once he got there. Of equal importance are the lessons he learned along the way, which can now be passed on to you.

YOU AND TIM

In 1998, at age 55, Tim sold his company and retired. After he had paid taxes on his income from the sale, his life savings stood at $12 million. I asked him how he was going to invest it.

He said, "Well, I'm going to take 33 percent of it and put it in U.S. T-bills." (At that time Treasury bills were paying a state tax-free rate of 5 percent.) He continued, "Then I'm going to take another 33 percent and put it in . . . U.S. T-bills. The rest I'm going to put in . . . U.S. T-bills!"

I laughed, but I was a bit shocked, since he had certainly

seemed to enjoy investing his money throughout the years I had known him. He had expensive tastes, and tended to spend many hundreds of thousands of dollars a year just on him and his wife.

I said, "What if someone comes along with a great investment idea?"

He said, "I'll tell them what I just told all five of my brokers: 'I don't need to play anymore. Go away, I'm done.'"

He explained that despite their love of travel and antique jewelry and fine art, he and his wife could never spend the amount of after-tax interest they would make annually from the T-bills. A very generous family budget filled with vacations and new cars and the like came to about $300,000 a year. That was all they needed with both of their kids already out of college and their house completely paid off.

They would ladder the remainder of the interest income back into whatever the current T-bill rate was. Over the long term he felt that should cover future inflationary trends beyond the original principal of $12 million.

Of course, it is possible to reach the End Game *with a lot less savings* by simply spending less per year than Tim and his wife.

Tim's goal was not to touch the original principal; which would be given to their two children when both Tim and his wife were gone. Their two children would inherit $6 million each, plus whatever gains on the interest Tim and his wife had not spent on themselves.

He felt he had been a good father and his wife was a great mother. They had taught their children well. His children would have to be responsible for the economic, creative, and spiritual teachings of *their* children.

Tim said, "If my two kids don't suddenly turn into bums and stop working altogether—which they won't—they will have plenty of money for themselves and their children. My grandchildren are then going to have to be responsible for their children's financial future, not me."

At that moment I had a revelation: He had won a game I had previously thought was endless and therefore not winnable!

He had made it without becoming a billionaire. By creating slightly altered game rules (declaring he would not be fiscally responsible for generations of unborn children—*the children of his grandchildren*) he had accumulated enough financial firepower at this point in the wealth accumulation process to not have to play the game anymore.

On New Year's Day 2000, Tim was sitting at a table with some close friends of his and they were all telling their stories about how some of their mutual funds had made 180 percent in 1999. They turned to Tim and asked, "How did you do last year?" He said, "I made 5 percent. And I'm glad you guys hit the jackpot. But let's talk in a few years and see who ends up with the best performance."

Of course, it didn't take long for each of his friends, and almost all traditional investors worldwide, to suffer losses of 30 to 70 percent in their portfolios during the 2000–2002 bear market.

This is not a story most brokers or financial advisers would want to tell. After all, they can't make a living selling you U.S. T-bills. And they would love you to believe that diversification itself will save you from disaster. But that is not at all guaranteed, as we will see in Chapter 4.

The truth is, at some point in your financial life, it may be that *any* traditional investment strategy, including diversifying into corporate bonds, carries risks you can no longer afford to take.

Horribly crazy, overly conservative ideas like the End Game strategy rock Wall Street to its core.

After all, how are all the brokers and advisers and hedge fund managers going to survive if the biggest players in the world don't want to play?

What would Wall Street do without all of its richest gunslingers throwing huge sums of money onto the casino's roulette wheel?

If you were to quit investing in a risky manner upon reaching the End Game, what would happen to *them?*

The hype-masters—the TV analysts, newsletter writers, investment magazines, investment web sites, and all the so-called experts on the Street—would certainly not like you very much anymore. They probably wouldn't agree with you, or this book. They would march a hundred pages of statistics in front of you about buy-and-hold strategies over the long term, emphasize the safety of diversification, and warn you about inflation eating away at your assets, to try to prove you wrong.

But you and Tim simply won't care anymore.

If you *did* care, you could spar with them with the statistics listed in Chapter 4. But I can tell you for sure, Tim wouldn't bother wasting his time.

You may ask, "But what about foreign currencies to protect against the possible fall of the U.S. dollar?" Glad you asked! This would be a clever question posed by those ready and willing to transact these investments for you for a fee.

Currencies are government paper. Is government paper outside the United States intrinsically safer and/or worth more than U.S. dollars? The short answer is: not for my money. Over the long term, my guess is that the dollar will weaken and strengthen at intervals impossible to time versus other currencies. If the U.S. dollar were permanently weakened, all currencies would be in a tumultuous situation. The U.S. dollar has been the de facto international currency since 1974; some would even say since shortly after World War II. In my opinion, this fact about U.S. currency will not be changing anytime in the foreseeable future.

You may ask: Why not invest in the traditional conservative programs that most brokers and financial planners offer?

The answer is: Traditional investment models do not offer enough growth for the protection they offer.

Also, there is no guarantee you won't lose a literal fortune in an unforeseen crisis. During these times they will tell you the loss is "statistically unexplainable." But all statistics they or you look at are backward looking. They are very rarely accurate predictive tools.

Big corporations *can* fail. In fact, they can fail quickly in dark times—WorldCom and Enron are two examples of mega-corporations that failed at lightning speed in 2002, and whose stocks eventually went to zero. Many hundreds of dot-com stocks, now known as "not.com" or "dot-bomb" stocks, failed within a few short months as well, after having become everyone's darlings. Even some "value" managers had some of these dot-com stocks in their portfolios, and held them all through the ride down.

Remember, 2002 was by no means a bad year in the economy. We were in a mild recession, not a depression. Things could have gotten far worse—worse than Japan's depression in the 1990s. Traditional investors who lost 30 to 50 percent of their life savings in times like these can consider themselves historically lucky! (See Part Two: Knowing the Difference between Market Stats and Market Hype.)

Yet, if these losses happened to you, "lucky" would not be the first word that would enter your mind. Neither would the phrase "Be patient." (This is what your adviser would be telling you.)

When using traditional investment strategies, patience may indeed pay off when things go badly if your patience spans years, or sometimes decades. But there are times when patience only leads to more losses.

How will you be able to know the difference between when patience will lead to success and when it will financially destroy you? Is it really worth it to spend years of your life waiting to find out which of the two outcomes will happen to you?

In my opinion, it isn't.

That is why over time traditional investing approaches do not work for the average investor. When risks are running high and losses become steeper by the day, too often even your advisers will tell you to change your portfolio to something more conservative— usually right near the lows of a cycle!

Very few advisers, at the peak of fear and panic, will tell you to "buy the dot-coms now; they're cheap." But those advisers who did suggest that, or scooped up Enron at $10 or WorldCom at $3, were dead wrong. You would have ended up with stock certificates of bankrupt companies—something to use as wallpaper for your basement, if you still had enough money left to pay the mortgage.

Therefore, we must find alternative investing strategies that can beat the casino at its own game. They *do* exist. We will explore them in the coming chapters.

But first we must make sure you have enough knowledge and discipline to be successful. That is why the emotional component is critical right from the start.

Having an end goal—a point where the game is over and you are declared the winner—is also a critical component. Those who go to casinos know that if they go back again and again, eventually the casino will wipe them out, no matter how much money they may have previously won.

Of course, most people are not yet within reach of the End Game. Still, each of us should learn the lessons the End Game has to offer *before we get there.*

We need to be fully aware that at best money can be a stepping-stone to a secure and happy life. At worst, it can turn into an assassin.

A business or investment failure can turn your self-image to mud. In contrast, the victories can overinflate your importance in the world.

You may begin to take risks just for the high they give you, or to make up for past losses you're still angry about.

As soon as this happens *the game is running you.*

True financial security does not always come to those who spend their entire lives focused on building a bigger and bigger empire. At some point, more money is not the point, and the empire itself is not the point.

Of course, we must oversee our finances and be ever vigilant. Of course, we all want to leave our children and other loved ones a secure future.

But the ultimate goal of the End Game is not to win it all. That goal is in fact a losing strategy. You and the ones you love will be the ultimate losers, regardless of the amount of money you amass, because the odds are very high that you will not be there for your own victory party. You will have no time to fully enjoy your hard work and good fortune. Instead you'll still be out there day after day winning and losing battles long after the war is over.

Truly understanding the End Game will bring us to the same conclusion Dr. Falcon's computer came to in the movie *War Games*. When challenged to beat itself in a game of tic-tac-toe, it went through a million games in two minutes, with each game ending in a tie. The computer then came to a revelation about the game (and about the "game" of thermonuclear war as well). It came to the End Game.

The computer-generated voice said over the NORAD loudspeaker: "Strange game, Dr. Falcon. It seems the only way to win is: not to play."

"Not to play" in the context of this book means that we commit ourselves to creating a portfolio that hedges risk first and foremost, and that we never again succumb to gambling our money away—even if the reward seems great. We know how much is enough. We are not interested in beating the stock market every year, or having more money than our richest friend or neighbor.

As soon as we grasp that key principle, we can then allow ourselves the freedom to look beyond the End Game even before we get there, and find out what else life has to offer.

2

Investing for Your Life versus Spending Your Life Investing

When the market says to an investor: "Your money or your life," most investors end up surrendering both.

WHAT DO YOU REALLY WANT?

After reading the preceding chapter, perhaps Donald Trump or George Soros come to mind and you are saying, "Yes, but they are still playing!" Okay, fair enough. Let's say for a moment that you want to be like them. (Bill Gates and Warren Buffett have apparently abandoned the game of endlessly accumulating money to some degree by giving vast sums to charity, so we'll stick with the ones still playing.)

Let's assume you have a unique passion and instinct like they do. Let's go a step further and say that playing the game of business, investing, and finance, and accumulating great material wealth *is* the only thing you want! Okay, then, your wish is my command.

I am often reminded of the myth of King Midas. He was granted one wish, remember? He wished that everything he touched could turn to gold. His walls turned to gold with the touch of his finger. That was fun! But then his hamburger turned to gold, his girlfriend turned to gold, his surfboard turned to gold (not very seaworthy but great car roof art). And, well, much to the chagrin of the Donald Trumps and Scrooges everywhere, King Midas was soon a mental goner.

Be careful of what you wish for! You have no idea how bad things can be once you get it!

For example, let's say you're really, really rich. You have inherited the late King Midas' estate. You now have $50 million, after tax!

Most of us would immediately want a fancy car, or three—a red Bentley convertible, perhaps? Or a Maserati? And a big house, in fact a mansion; yes, and maybe a private plane and a yacht— all the things that multimillion-dollar, and billion-dollar, fortune makers seem to want and have. They can buy all of these things without giving the money a second thought. You want the same toys.

Go buy them (hypothetically for now).

But let me ask you some very mundane questions: How are you going to take care of all these things, maintain them, store them, and keep them safe? How much time is it going to take to research which car and plane and boat and house is best for you? Certainly, you could afford to hire someone, or a staff of people, to research and choose and maintain and find security for all these things. But who will manage that staff? Who manages the staff manager? Who oversees their expense budgets and payrolls? Who oversees the overseers with access to your primary bank accounts?

It gets complicated. It gets time-consuming. Trusting people, even old friends, may become an issue. (And you'll have lots of new friends to mistrust!)

I have many wealthy clients who live unhappy, complicated lives *because* of their material possessions. I am amazed at the amount of time they spend just maintaining, upgrading, and learning about their endless new toys.

COWS

There is a story told about Buddha and the burden of material passions:

Buddha was sitting in a field meditating with several students. A farmer came rushing up to the group waving his hands and crying out:

"Oh, sirs, forgive me for interrupting you but I am in dire need of your help. You see, I have spent my entire life raising cows. And yesterday one of the cows broke through my fence. The rest followed! And they are now scattered all across this valley, lost or hiding. I must find them or my life will turn tragic and I might die poor. I might even starve to death someday! Have any one of you seen any cows come this way?"

Buddha calmly looked at the man and said, "I am so sorry, sir, but we have seen no cows pass this way, I assure you."

The farmer was stunned at his bad luck. He said, "Well, if you *do* see any cows, please be sure to contact me right away. I live right there across the valley between those two hills, at least for now. If I do not find my cows I may not have that house for long." At this thought his face went rigid with fear. Then he suddenly ran off in another direction looking for his cows, his arms flailing.

Buddha told everyone to close their eyes, and after a long meditation he said to his students:

"We must all be so very thankful . . . that none of us have any cows."

Possessions are like sacred cows. They often cause more grief than they are worth on any level.

It's ironic that a rich person might lord over his financial empire, only to become enslaved by his own possessions.

Many of my wealthy investors daydream with me about their college days when they were free of things. They fondly recall living in a messy dorm room; hanging out with friends listening to the Beatles, or the Rolling Stones, or Jimi Hendricks; playing co-ed tag football on the quad before dinner.

It makes you stop and wonder . . .

WHAT WOULD ACTUALLY MAKE YOU *FEEL* RICH?

I am blessed to be living in Maui, Hawaii. For 30 years I lived in Marin County, California. Marin is a very beautiful place. We owned a beautiful house. We had very beautiful friends. We had plenty of money. But there were some drawbacks as well. Winters are long and rainy. Many people adore the more moderate temperatures in the summer there. I was not one of them. I like to play tennis on a hot, wind-free day. I like bodysurfing in a clean, shell-free tropical ocean.

Just before my 50th birthday, my wife said to me: "Something still seems like it's missing for you. You love me and the kids, and we are living far more comfortably than when we first met, beyond our wildest dreams, in fact, but you are not enjoying your day-to-day life as much as you should. You seem a little down sometimes."

Then she asked the oddest thing: "What would make you feel rich?"

Understand, at that point we were already statistically rich, so it wasn't about me responding with some dollar figure.

I thought about it and said: "What would make me feel rich

would be living where we vacation, so I don't have to wait for those few times a year to relax and love my surroundings; living in Maui, near a beach, in the sun, in a Spanish-style house, but not one that's too big!" (I had already made the mistake of living in a house that was too big for my taste. I needed a cell phone to find my family in some other part of the house.) I like to hear my kids laughing or crying from another room, and to smell what's on the stove for dinner.

I continued: "I'd like to be able to walk on the beach every day, and play tennis all year round. Then we could vacation on the mainland and visit friends and family in the summer. That's what would make me feel rich, even if we never accumulated another dime beyond what we have now."

The other part of this story is that once we moved here and observed the various lifestyles of the locals, something curious struck me:

The surfers.

Their morning, and their life, begins when the surf is up. (And I mean up, since the waves at "Jaws" can get to be about 50 feet high.) Some of these surfers are 18 or 19 years old. Some are over 30. They are strong and ocean-tested. Many live in boarding-houses for a few hundred dollars a month, sleeping on mattresses on the floor. They drive $800 cars, eat two meals a day when they have the time, party late into the night, and work a few days a week to earn the money they need for their very modest expenses: surf-board wax and the like.

They don't apply for welfare. They don't think anyone owes them anything. They are not worried about their retirement. They wouldn't know what to do with a stock certificate.

Are they poor? Or are they rich?

They are not "high net worth." But are they as rich as I am? Or are they maybe even *extremely* rich?

Sometimes when I am in a store eyeing some $5,000 piece of furniture, images of surfers out there chasing the next wave haunt me. Sometimes the images do their job and put my life in perspective. I walk out of the furniture store wondering why I would have even considered buying another thing in my already too-cluttered life. What hallucination had overcome me? Did I need to fulfill some static image of the perfect home, or a perfect life, that badly? And was buying something new for the living room the way to get it? Sometimes I wonder if the surfers haven't just gone right to the End Game without even passing through the rest of the financial maze to get there.

The things money can't buy—true love, free time, a lack of stress, having a sense of wonder about life, or having a calling that makes your life worth living—all these things can often get further and further out of reach even as your bank account grows.

Therefore, we must make it our primary business to succeed at managing our own personal life.

All the other business we conduct should be seen as a series of subsidiaries to this one key umbrella company—our life.

THE BOTTOM-LINE QUESTION

Here is the critical question, *on a pure business level:*

How do you secure your financial future, while at the same time increasing your sense of joy and fulfillment?

The answer is to choose only risk-averse investments for your portfolio, and to therefore spend less time and energy riding the waves of great wins and heavy losses.

With the free time that becomes available to you from choosing less volatile, less market-correlated investments, and *not* having to chase the latest craze and hottest returns (which statistically is a failed strategy), you dare to go and live your life.

Buy a board. Learn to surf . . . you name it.

3

The Power of Hedging

Always Hedge Your Bets

HEDGING STEP 1: GIVING UP THE WINDFALL TO AVOID THE BIG FALL

A good investor's mantra should be the same as the title of the old Firesign Theater comedy album from long ago: "Everything You Know Is Wrong."

Too many people, especially after achieving great entrepreneurial success, are thrown into the world of investing without a clue. Being entrepreneurs, they often feel that if they were successful in one business, they can be successful in the business of investing. How hard can it be? So they try and fail, or worse, succeed initially and then fail on a far bigger scale, never realizing the difference between investing and gambling. By the time they find out how enormous the risks are it's often too late.

Other investors think they know what the next hot stock or sector is going to be. They rely on tips from a TV pundit, or their broker, or a friend, not realizing that by the time they've heard it, millions of institutional investors have long ago placed their bets and are now waiting to sell to the highest bidder. By the time this news has reached CNBC or your friend or the financial press, it has entered into the speculation phase. This is when an investor must rely on his or her mantra rather than the "can't fail" advice being fed to them on a silver platter. Repeat after me: "Everything you know is wrong."

Other investors are desperate to catch up. They have endured devastating losses, humiliating losses due to bad advice or bad judgment, or losses incurred from a bear market despite being "diversified." These investors are now willing to take big gambles with their remaining dollars (like chips at the casino) to recover their losses.

The problem is that the casino's job is to wipe you out. Time is on the casino's side. It is as patient as a rattlesnake. It's a mean game played by very wizened odds makers. You are on the other side of the table.

HOW CAN YOU AVOID SERIOUS LOSSES? EMOTIONAL HEDGES

Most of the world's great investors will tell you the best way to make money is not to lose it. I would add that the best way to make money on a consistent basis is not to make inconsistent money.

Aggressive investing of any kind creates inconsistent money. Win big, lose big. In a way it's like a vacuum. That vacuum, which needs to be filled, sucks in not only your dollar bills in search of the Holy Grail (the big investment idea that will set you free) but also your emotions, your time, and your mental focus day to day, and sometimes hour to hour.

There is a company no one knows about yet; buy its stock for pennies on the dollar and when it goes public, you'll be rich.

No, no, short the dollar.

Buy gold.

Buy oil.

Short cattle futures.

Its nanotech, stupid. Don't you see? (A cogent explanation follows. . . .)

Put everything you have into real estate. It'll never go down.

Which one of these investing ideas is the slot machine that's ready to spit out millions of dollars when you pull the handle?

The answer is too often: none of the above.

It can get very confusing unless you have a disciplined strategy that bypasses a good deal of the risk and decision making. That discipline is what I call "the psychology of hedging."

A hedge is playing one risk or opportunity against another risk or opportunity, which when combined increases the opportunity while it decreases the risk.

Hedging was the methodology introduced in the original Jones model. Alfred Winslow Jones, a sociologist, created the first hedge fund in 1949. Hedge funds were dissected and defined for decades according to how closely they aligned their methodologies with the Jones model.

The idea behind the Jones model was to buy stocks of great companies that you thought had value at their present selling price, and simultaneously short (bet against the rise of) stocks of companies you thought were bad companies and overvalued—in equal dollar amounts.

That left your account or portfolio "market direction neutral," or "dollar neutral." Theoretically, because you hedged out directionality from the market itself, the astuteness of your ideas would make you money whether the market went up or down.

As time proved, life and the markets aren't quite simple

enough, or static enough, to allow any one strategy to work for long. Not even the Jones model.

Why?

The reason is that all models (including those based on modern portfolio theory) eventually lose their ability to take advantage of the natural inefficiencies they originally discovered, because once enough people become aware of those inefficiencies, the market suddenly becomes very efficient in that way. The window of opportunity closes like a door to another dimension.

Therefore, every model and strategy has to be hedged with other models and strategies. **Every investment, no matter how good, will eventually be efficiently valued,** and therefore must be hedged with other investments and/or asset classes, in case market efficiency begins to neutralize the alpha (the beyond average investment growth) of the original strategy.

Such has been the evolution of the hedge fund world itself: The concept of hedging has now morphed into thousands of different, sometimes successful, species of hedge funds. Understanding hedge funds can be daunting. Investing in them can be either very fulfilling or downright dangerous. (I discuss hedge funds in far more detail in future chapters.)

But there are also *emotional* hedges that go hand in hand with the investment hedges.

Emotional hedges are critical to all investors at every stage of their investment life.

Let me give you an example of an emotional hedge:

Let's say you feel real estate values are bound to fall over the next few years. The financial press has begun to talk about the real estate bubble, and interest rates are rising. You own two houses. You've made quite a windfall in both properties. But now you are thinking about taking your profits and waiting for better value a few years down the road.

Choice A: Sell neither house. In fact, buy another one. If there is a speculative bubble you want to make sure you participate in the final blow-out phase. Sell your other investments to get the liquidity for a down payment and buy a third property. Maybe those friends who are telling you real estate in your area will never go down are right.

Choice B: Be a value investor. Sell at the top and buy at the bottom. Everyone who is logical knows this is a bubble. No one can time the top of the market perfectly. Take the profits now and run! Sell both houses while you still have a chance to cash in. Rent a nice apartment until the bubble breaks, and then go in like a vulture and cherry-pick the best properties at the best values. Within 10 years you will be very rich indeed.

Let's analyze each choice:

Choice A: You may indeed make even more money than you have already. Maybe you can even sell before the sky falls. It's painful to watch everyone else becoming richer and richer while you play it conservatively all the time.

However, if you are wrong, you could lose so much money on all three houses that it might wipe out all the years of profits you had made in the two original houses and then some.

Choice B: You sell everything now and wait out the storm. Living in an apartment isn't such a bad idea for a while. The idea of downsizing feels like a relief. There are no roof leaks to pay for. No ownership hassles. No property tax. Then when the time is right you will become a real estate baron. You'll make a windfall and be set for life.

However, if you are wrong and property values continue to rise, you might not be able to get back into the housing market safely at some point down the road when prices have doubled yet again.

Which choice is the right one?

None of the above.

I try to hedge every investment and business move I make. So I would choose choice C.

Choice C: Keep the house I want to live in. Sell the other. The result: Either I win, or I win bigger!

If the housing market continues to rise, the house I'm living in will rise with it. So I win.

If the housing market crashes, or at least goes down to a level where value is created, I will have cash available from the sale of the second home to buy another house at a discount to what the asking price is at present, so I will win even bigger over time.

Both outcomes in choice C are good. I have hedged my bet, hedged my risk, and set myself up to be emotionally fulfilled with either outcome.

(Or, if the housing market stays flat for five years, that's fine, too. With choice C, time is on my side.)

HEDGING STEP 2: DIVERSIFICATION

The most common hedge in investing and business is diversification: spreading out your assets into many different investments.

The key reason diversification works is that with investments being intrinsically risky, and often volatile, patience is key.

We cannot emotionally or fiscally afford to wait and pray as our investment continues to lose value if it represents too much of our net worth or emotional currency.

Conversely, if we do not need the money, if our life will not change if the investment goes down substantially, we can afford to wait to see if our initial instinct about that investment was right.

Diversification must help your overall portfolio to stay relatively steady over a series of investment horizons and economic cycles. Unless you can devise a successful systematic timing strategy (which very few investors have ever accomplished), the odds are the market will defeat your logic, your natural instincts, insights, and attempted manipulations. That's what makes the market

so dangerous. Therefore, diversifying the ideas, asset classes, and strategies in your portfolio is crucial for long-term success.

ENDEAVOR NOT TO INVEST MORE THAN YOU ARE EMOTIONALLY AND FINANCIALLY ABLE TO LOSE IN ANY SINGLE INVESTMENT

Imagine losing 100 percent of the money you invested in this single idea. How would that feel? It may happen. Why risk more than you can financially lose?

Additionally, it's not smart to bankroll your own business venture with more money than you can afford to lose. You must assume it could fail before a single dollar of your investment is recovered. The odds are high that a start-up business will fail. Very few start-ups ever see a profit, regardless of how good the concept behind the business is. You may have a vision that is spectacular. But the crafts of finding cheap manufacturing, engaging a good distributor, and knowing how to neutralize or eliminate the competition must all fall into place as well. Otherwise, your venture will likely fall into one of the many thousands of traps that await each innocent and unprotected artistic vision.

HEDGING STEP 3: LOGIC OF THE MIND IS NOT THE ONLY KIND

There is another type of emotional hedge.

It hedges out our tendency to rely solely on the mind for money and business decisions.

But it's more than relying on just the heart. Instead we create a hedge, or a synergy, between the two.

Ever since Plato, rational thought and logic have become the totem of, and in many ways the definition of, civilization. Logical thinking has been revered for more than 20 centuries.

From rational thinking and searing logic, scientific methods have been devised, investment strategies have found their edge, rockets and bombs and the Big Bang have all become part of reality. And here we are, the sons and daughters of Plato's time, still searching for the meaning of life and the road to peace after all these thousands of years of logic.

In my view, a complete sense of reason can be accessed only through combining it with things like personal integrity, alliance building, and an openness to entirely different ways of assessing the truth. There is a wisdom and an expertise that comes from that kind of emotional control.

This, I contend, is a well-kept secret in the financial world.

In a strange way, when money and investing are not seen as either a burden or a final objective in life, success becomes easier to come by.

Here are a few quick examples of what might occur when a deeper sense of "emotional logic" is employed:

You are not tricked into bad investments or business decisions out of a feeling of desperation, envy, or greed.

Competitors may be willing to affiliate with you and combine their strengths with yours because they trust your intentions.

Your most valuable employees may be far more loyal to you than to another employer because they know you care as much about them as you care about making a profit.

Better yet, you financially incentivize your most valuable and loyal employees so that you both have the same goals of growing the company.

THE GAMBLER'S CATCH-22

In the financial world, carefully choosing diversified investments, and hedging your emotions, as well as your assets, against failure and the unforeseen, is what I call investing. The rest I call gambling.

Addiction to the gambling element—not having your greed checked or your fears honored—turns the best-intentioned and smartest of people into neurotics.

The burden becomes more intense every day. And then the strangest thing happens. Your mind often creates a trap, a catch-22 so seemingly logical that you are lost for years on its wave as it pulls you deeper and deeper out to sea.

Here is an example of the gambler's catch-22:

Let's say you are trying to time the sale of an investment you don't plan to own for life.

Every time the investment is rising in price you say, "Why should I sell it now? It has momentum—it's bound to go up some more." Every time it falls to a point of concern you say, "Well, I can't sell it now, not until I make back some of the money I just lost. Then I'll sell it." But then if it rises to the place that you promised yourself you'd sell it, you go back to: "Why should I sell it now? It has momentum—it's bound to go up some more."

So then, when exactly do you sell? You are caught in the gambler's catch-22.

What's frightening is how easily investing can become an addiction even for people who are not originally drawn to play the game. Online brokers sell you on $5 trades. The financial media make you feel foolish for not buying the hottest trend. Numbers running on the bottom of a screen can destroy your financial life or make you massively wealthy in nanoseconds. No sense of reality is left. Dangers come fast and unforeseen.

How, then, do you play the investing game rather than it playing you? How do you prevent yourself from waking up one day and finding yourself gambling with your retirement money? This is when your focus and attention on the End Game become critical.

With each investment, and with your entire portfolio of

investments, setting up financial and emotional hedges will be the key to your long-term success.

No one trade, no one asset class, and no one system will remain inefficient and profitable forever. There *is no* permanent edge you can achieve. When the masses enter the game, the game has begun its death spiral.

Therefore:

☞ Don't invest more than you are comfortable losing in any one investment idea.

☞ Don't invest all your money in only one or even two asset classes like stocks, bonds, commodities, or real estate.

☞ Find a way to hedge every investment decision you make—like the previous housing example.

☞ Never put yourself in a position where the game can play you, as in the gambler's catch 22.

☞ Stay hedged emotionally.

☞ Always have sell stops in mind (levels where you will bail out on the losing side of a trade and where you will sell a winning trade), each marked by a set price, before you make an investment.

No doubt investing is the way to secure your future if you play the game safely and carefully. This new paradigm of hedging your bets in both the economic and emotional dimensions will set up a road map for success.

Here is what you must continuously ask yourself to avoid the addictions and the traps of the investing game:

"Do I want to be the CEO of a money management firm?"

If so, get your license and find clients. If not, then don't try to be one.

Here is my definition of the stock market (and, in fact, all capital markets):

People trying to outfox people trying to outfox them.

If you think you can be the Chief Fox, that is well and good. But don't think you can outfox some of the most cunning manipulators in the world with ease or on a part-time basis.

Now let's continue doing some due diligence on the markets, and come face-to-face with the dark side of the promised land.

Part Two

KNOWING THE DIFFERENCE BETWEEN MARKET STATS AND MARKET HYPE

4

Just the Facts, Ma'am

MARKET FORECASTING AND TIMING

"Sometimes the magic works, sometimes it doesn't."
— *The Chief from the movie* Little Big Man

Despite enormous risks and volatility, it is hard to find anything that has beaten the growth in the U.S. stock market over long periods of time.

For instance, from 1980 to 2006, despite housing bubbles in some regions of the country in the current decade, the stock market has dwarfed the profits made from real estate.

Your local stockbroker will be quick to tell you that patient investors will earn about 10 percent a year annually "over the long haul." (That figure is actually closer to 5 percent for the average investor over the past 100 years, according to John Mauldin's book, *Just One Thing* [John Wiley & Sons, 2005].)

The other problem with the 10 percent a year theory has been volatility:

☞ In 1973–1974 there was a decline of 45 percent in the Standard & Poor's (S&P) 500 index. It took well over 10 years for an

S&P-weighted portfolio to recover its losses and finally break even.

☞ During the 14-year period from 1968 to 1982, the S&P fell about 20 percent.

☞ Since 1929 there have been 10 major bear markets—an average of about one every seven years. The average bear market loss was about 41 percent.

☞ There have been 39 years of secular bear market periods in the past 77 years.

☞ During the 2000–2002 bear market, the S&P fell 49 percent from its highs in March of 2000. The NASDAQ was down close to 80 percent from its March 2000 highs.

During the period 1929–1932, the Dow Jones Industrial Average lost approximately **19, 32, 54, and 19 percent** in four consecutive years!

To minimize volatility, many investors have tried market timing. Others have tried trading systems they have seen on TV, while still others have tried investing according to the predictions of a particular financial guru or newsletter.

I study many systems and have analyzed previously successful financial newsletters. Unfortunately, since the end of what was known as international arbitrage in 2003, the performances of timing system strategies have not been good. Many, including myself, continue to search for the Holy Grail of market timing strategies. But real-time performance numbers over the life of the strategy urge caution. Systems offered on TV are for the most part completely misleading. And as far as the newsletters are concerned, they work until they don't. And when they fail, many tend to fail in a rather dramatic way.

Here are two of my favorite quotes in the financial world:

We have two classes of forecasters: Those who don't know . . .
and those who don't know they don't know.
　　　　　　　　　　　　　　　—John Kenneth Galbraith

For those who try to follow momentum signals or use logic-driven systems, price-earnings (P/E) ratios, or valuation-based models, consider this quote:

> *The market can stay irrational longer than you can remain solvent.*
>
> —John Maynard Keynes

Though it might be best to let these quotes speak for themselves, I will put it less eloquently.

☞ No forecaster I know of gets it right with enough consistency to make their opinion valuable.

☞ Anything based on back-tests is almost never worth the paper that the fabulous returns are written on.

☞ Anyone trying to sell supposedly successful trading systems on radio or TV or by a seminar is a kook at best, a crook at worst. If the system worked they would not be sipping tea with you in a meeting room in Kansas. They would be billionaires with no use for you whatsoever.

☞ No one is putting on a seminar to be kind to you. If they *did* want to do it out of kindness they would certainly not charge money for it at any step along the way. Why would they need money when their trading system can just about manufacture money anytime they want it? And *why* would they tell the world about it? Because:

☞ If everyone used the same system to trade, it wouldn't work anymore. They would have killed the Golden Goose. Trading systems can work only by exploiting inefficiencies.

HIGHER RISK TOO OFTEN EQUALS LESS REWARD

Taking risk without knowing and understanding the investment itself in a very deep way, and without understanding the process of risk taking itself, vastly decreases the possibility of reward by the time you sell your position.

Aggressive investments left to chance, or time, will too often turn into losses. And it's very tough to make your money back, or even want to play anymore, when you're down 30 or 50 percent. (See section later in the chapter called "The Secret Poison: Losses Overwhelm Gains.")

The most important question to ask is: Why risk?

Ask yourself why you "love" a certain investing idea, or stock, or fund, or asset class like gold or real estate. If when you are honest with yourself the answer is because it is at present making money, then know your "love" is very likely based on something more akin to gambling, not investment logic.

Your odds of profiting in the future from this investment idea have also decreased to the level of a gambler's odds. When this "love" lets you down and causes you financial heartbreak, you will likely leave it with anger, and leave it as a loser.

A great investor doesn't say, "I love this stock or asset class; therefore I will invest" or "therefore I will invest more." He or she says, "No matter how successful I think this can be, how can I hedge my risks?"

Avoid putting yourself in a position where you can lose more than a small percentage of *any investment* at any point along the way, *starting at this present point*, regardless of when you bought it.

Assess what your portfolio of assets looks like today. No regrets. No love addictions.

Rearrange it, synchronize it, into one *synergistic hedge*.

Each part of the whole should also be hedged. Do not play around with the outer fringes of your assets. The losses incurred can ruin an otherwise good year or good portfolio. This is one way higher risk can often lead to less reward.

This powerful mind-set is for wealthy investors, *not* because it doesn't work for the other investors, but because:

Wealthy investors who follow this rule stay wealthy.

Wealthy investors who ignore this mind-set slowly or quickly join the ranks of "the other investors."

WHAT IS TRUE DIVERSIFICATION?

Playing with the stock market is like playing chicken with a freight train . . . no matter how many times you win, you only get to lose once.

—Mike Masters

The most commonly known way to hedge a portfolio is to diversify the investments. However, when all the investments are based on the upward trends of various markets or stocks or the fiscal safety of corporate bonds or foreign countries, then diversification actually *decreases.*

Why? Because all of your assets are betting on uptrends and/or the well-being of the global landscape. And neither are reliable bets.

Underestimating the difficulty of diversifying a portfolio is very common. But the *biggest* mistake investors can make is betting their financial futures on a single stock, sector, concentrated theme, or asset class (that includes the darlings of generations past and present—gold and real estate).

Even bonds have volatile cycles and trends, despite their often tepid annual returns.

Investors usually make the assumption that they will have the staying power to wait out bear market losses in their investments. But that waiting period often takes many years; sometimes it takes many decades. During that time, individuals and families often lose fortunes.

Very few investors have the financial or psychological capability to sustain themselves during those violent down cycles. The average secular bear market in the U.S. equity market in the twentieth century was 17 years.

During the years 2000 through 2002, many investors found their 401(k) and private portfolios incurring serious losses of 20 percent to 50 percent of their assets, despite thinking they were safely diversified with a mix of bonds and equities.

Importantly, if the next bear market is an inflation-generated bear market, bonds could lose a great deal of their principal and/or not keep up with inflation. Although noncorporate bonds saved some investors from total disaster in 2000 to 2002, they may not save those investors next time.

Every bear market has a different set of booby traps. It is almost impossible to set up a traditional portfolio that prevents serious losses when bear market cycles run their course.

Here is a list of diversified indexes and asset classes that were all down from their historic 1999 or 2000 highs by the end of 2002.

Russell Small Cap Index −36%
Dow Jones Industrial Average −38%
S&P 500 −49%
NASDAQ −78%
Gold Index −64%
Biotech Index −66%
European Index −63%
Asia Index −58%
Brazil −58%
Argentina −70%
China−52%
India −58%
Japan −61%

How do the wealthy truly diversify while staying invested for growth? By hedging against directional market risk with a well-diversified mix of noncorrelated hedge fund strategies, such as:

☞ Asset-based lending.
☞ Structured financing, such as mortgage-backed loans, collateralized debt obligations (CDOs), collateralized mortgage obligations (CMOs), and asset-backed securities (ABSs).
☞ Various forms of options trading.
☞ Fixed income trading.
☞ Real estate–related loans and special situations.
☞ Global macro trading.
☞ Private investments in public equity (PIPEs).

Do not invest in any single investment offered to you in these strategies. Always invest with a well due diligenced, experienced hedge fund manager that has a diversified portfolio of the above investments, or better yet, find a successful fund of funds that invests in these strategies.

Following past performance—the hot fund, sector, or asset class—from year to year, or month to month, is statistically a losing strategy.

THE TWO GREAT MYTHS
OF TRADITIONAL INVESTING

The Buy-and-Hold Myth

Don't tell me how much money you made in a bull market; tell me how much of it you got to keep at the bottom of a bear market.

> —Veteran mutual fund manager to a young
> manager who reported a 120 percent gain
> during the Internet boom in 1999

Buy-and-hold investing is bull market advertising. You won't hear anyone talking about it after the roof caves in. This is my humble opinion, based on my experience watching and listening to the vast majority of the financial media from the middle of 2000 through 2002. One by one, the buy-and-hold cheerleaders disappeared. (None of them disappeared soon enough to prevent major losses in their clients' accounts, though.)

For those continuing to espouse the value of "buy and hold," let's put this strategy in further historical perspective.

In 1973–1974, when the market lost 47 percent of its value, while banks were at the same time offering better than 15 percent returns on one-year certificates of deposit (CDs), few thought "buy and hold" was a smart idea. Nor would they if this situation were to occur again.

And no one can be sure that the years following a severe bear market won't continue to worsen, like the 1930s did after 1929 or as happened in 2002 after two years of already devastating declines.

The most realistic question to ask oneself as an investor is: Why invest in corporations when the macro-environment is not conducive to their success? Why not find alternatives until the environment changes?

A few examples: Why stay in a slowing sector of the economy or a company falling into possible bankruptcy or scandal, or stay in an asset class like gold (which everyone owned in their portfolios for decades, until—inexplicably at the time—it collapsed into a 20-year bear market), when you can make more money, and safer money, elsewhere?

Warren Buffett, the Most Famous of the Buy-and-Hold Investors, Isn't

Alarming but true for buy-and-hold advocates—Warren Buffett is not an investor in the stock market. His philosophy is not "buy and hold." His investing model is to personally dissect and analyze one company at a time, know the product, know the CEO and the board members, and invest if he thinks the personnel are exceptional and the stock is undervalued.

In other words, he is a venture capitalist of the highest order—a literal co-owner of companies that he finances, then personally helps direct by often sitting on the board.

When he sees fundamentals deteriorating within the company, he will sell his stock.

If he sees a recession looming, he will buy bonds to hedge his business investments.

In times of perceived inflation he has bought silver or gold, and then sold it when he perceives a change.

He shorted $20 billion against the U.S. dollar between 2003 and 2005, betting instead on other countries' currencies such as the euro. By the end of 2006 he was losing that bet.

Warren Buffett would never stay invested in a company simply to save himself from paying capital gains or any other types of taxes! (You can read more about that in the next section.)

He is simply a brilliant analyst and a shrewd horse trader. He is irreplaceable. No one can imitate what he does. By no means can Buffett be compared to a buy-and-hold investor, who chooses blue-chip companies to hold forever through the recommendations of a local stockbroker or by individual analysis.

Buffett indeed has handily beaten the stock market over time. But he has also endured extreme volatility along the way. Berkshire Hathaway, the proxy for what his company owns, lost approximately 24 percent of its value in 1998, recovered in 1999, only to lose approximately 45 percent thereafter. By the end of 2005, five years later, it had again recovered its losses.

Here's a clear example of how "buy and hold" can destroy a portfolio:

Anyone who bet in the early 1980s that personal computers were going to be all the rage was brilliantly insightful. But if that person had bought Commodore Computer and held it, he or she still would have lost every penny of the investment.

Of course, if at some point they had sold Commodore for a loss and switched to Dell Computer instead, they'd be up thousands of percent.

Bottom line: Do not believe in "buy and hold."

When it comes right down to it, few professional investors do.

The Secret Poison: Losses Overwhelm Gains

If you had been visionary enough to overweight the technology sector in 1999, you might have made 100 percent in your mutual fund holdings that year.

If, however, you believed in buy and hold, or in the abilities of mutual fund managers to protect you, you would have lost 50 to 80 percent from 2000 through 2002.

This scenario means that you, and all the other tech investors who believed in the "new paradigm," *lost* money throughout the multiyear period, even though you first earned 100 percent, and then lost "only" 50 to 80 percent in the following years.

Because:

When you make 100 percent and then lose 50 percent—all you do is break even.

When you make 100 percent and then lose 80 percent—you have a net loss of –60 percent.

Losses overwhelm gains. Therefore:

The key to great investing is to always protect your principal first and attempt to make a profit second.

The Tax Savings Myth

Pay Taxes, Be Happy (The Song Bobby McFerrin Was Afraid to Sing)

Countless times I have seen investors hold a stock, or limited partnership, or mutual fund, far beyond a time horizon they feel is risk appropriate simply to avoid paying taxes on the gains—*only to incur losses that far exceed what they tried to save in taxes.*

If you avoid selling even a great investment to delay the tax on the gains, by the time the sellers are in full swing you may not have a tax problem anymore, because all your gains may have been wiped out and replaced by net losses.

The key is to take the necessary steps to *protect* principal over any given market cycle.

Beware: Tax Compounding Can Work in Reverse

If you make money on your investment, tax compounding is indeed working for you. By delaying paying taxes and keeping that money invested, you make money on the delayed tax money. You are in fact leveraging your investment.

But in times of loss, it is leveraging your losses as well.

Tax compounding is simply a form of leverage, because whenever you finally do withdraw from a profitable investment, even if it's in 50 years, you will still pay a long-term capital gains tax on all your profits from the original investment.

If you pay tax on short-term gains each year, you would pay as you go. Two positive things would then occur:

1. You or your adviser would be free to sell any investment at any time.
2. You could take any and all investment losses off of future taxable gains with no time limit.

These advantages will not outweigh the mathematical benefits of tax-efficient investing in a bull market environment.

But over an entire economic cycle, the benefits of being able to find a safe harbor can *and do* psychologically and mathematically outweigh tax-efficient investing.

Long-term vision must include creating opportunities to negate risk, even if taxes have to be paid.

Conclusion

Tax efficiency of course must always be a factor in your investment decisions—especially *before* you invest.

(See the section later in the chapter called "Hedge Fund and Mutual Fund Taxes—Buyers Beware.")

But tax efficiency should hardly ever be your reason to hold on to an investment that you believe should be sold.

Do always check with your CPA to see what is the most tax-efficient way to sell.

There may be ways to shelter some of the tax.

But . . .

Trying to beat the Internal Revenue Service is "I.R.S." An irresponsible and risky strategy.

In bull markets, tax compounding using buy-and-hold strategies can work to your advantage. But you are simply leveraging the direction of the market, for better or for worse. (You can obtain margin loans at your local broker with the same result.)

This is the ultimate devil's bargain. You delay paying your taxes and you leverage your potential gains, but forfeiting your right to sell the investment may ultimately wipe out all of your past profits, and your original principal, too.

This is not a trade-off Warren Buffett or any other wise investor would ever make.

TAX CONFOUNDING: A STORY

A friend of mine, whom I will call Joe, sold his business to a larger firm in 1996. The firm paid him with 500,000 shares of stock. The good news was he could sell the stock right away. The bad news was it came with the tax basis at zero. That meant if he sold the stock he would have to pay a 20 percent capital gains tax on all the money he received from the sale.

When the firm purchased Joe's company, the stock was selling on the open market for $13. He therefore acquired 500,000 shares at a total current value of $6,500,000.

Before the sale of his company, Joe was cash poor. All of his money was tied up in his business and his house. Now with one phone call he could be flush with cash and could choose any number of ways to invest the money.

However, there was a problem. Joe hated the thought of paying taxes on $6,500,000. One-fifth of his gains would be wiped out just by selling the shares.

The other piece to the puzzle was that he felt certain that the stock was going to go up, and maybe even double. So why should he sell any of it?

I advised him that regardless of whether he wanted to pay the tax or thought the stock was going to go up, there was the right thing to do and the wrong thing to do. The wrong thing to do was to have a vast majority of his assets invested in any one stock, even if it was General Electric or Microsoft. But the fact that this was a relatively unknown company made it all the more risky. I told him, "Always be willing to pay your taxes. You'll have to someday." But I explained to him that it would be terrible to have to pay the same 20 percent tax on a stock that, God forbid, might some day be cut in half and selling at $6. The very illiquid nature of the stock might further erode the stock price if he tried to sell it all at once, especially during a time of panic.

Since there was no stock to short (too illiquid) and no puts or calls to hedge the position, I suggested he sell half of his shares right away and put stop limits on the rest, which could then be raised if the stock did go up from $13.

Joe appreciated my suggestion but assured me he was aware of the fiscal health and future plans of the company that had just acquired his firm. The CEO also expressed confidence that the company was expanding rapidly and growing its profit margins.

A month later the stock had fallen to $9. But Joe felt it was a mere blip. There was no way he was selling, especially since he had just lost 30 percent of his money, at least on paper.

A month after that the stock was at $16. He said to me, "My only regret is that I didn't buy more at $9."

He had now become trapped in the gambler's catch-22. "I can't sell it now, not until I've recouped my losses" or "Why would I sell it when it's going up? It's on a roll and is bound to go up further. (Besides, I am not going to pay that damn tax.)"

Tax compounding, in fact, was now his mantra. He did not see a reason to ever sell any stock as long as it wasn't a dog. Taxes were just too high. And the miracle of tax compounding was too compelling to be chased out of a stock just because it was going down temporarily. After all, it was as if he had another 20 percent worth of stock invested for free. When that stock made a 50 percent gain his extra 20 percent would make him an extra 10 percent net. He brought me charts on the miracles of tax compounding (that he has since thrown out).

Six months later the stock was at $6. Joe was contemplating buying more. I said, "You know, if you just look at it as a static event, without blaming yourself or panicking, what you have now, if you were to sell it today, is $3 million ($2.4 million after tax). That's a lot of money to have safely in a bank, and a lot of money to put at risk in one company at the present time—it represents most of your net worth."

Joe was now taking Advil twice a day and going to a chiropractor for his headaches. Nonetheless, he could not imagine giving up $600,000 to the government, even if it would mean getting himself out of this nightmare he was now living.

I once again suggested he might consider selling half. He said, predictably, "But then if it goes back to $13 or $16 I will have just been scared out. And I wouldn't be able to live with myself."

I said, "Can you live with yourself now?" At that point he was silent. I felt sorry for hurting his feelings. So I tried another route.

If You Had a Choice: Would You Presently Own It?

I said to Joe, "Let's pretend, whether the stock is up from here or down from here, that you are going to sell it at *some price* and pay the capital gains tax *someday*. Let's pretend you are not going to be trapped in this bet forever."

I continued, "Let's also pretend that you had a pile of after-tax cash sitting at your feet: $2,400,000, in fact, by total coincidence." I gave him a wink. Now he was smiling a bit.

"Let's have this cash, your cash, right next to you in thousand-dollar bills. The cash is 100 percent yours to do with what you wish. Now I have this stock you used to own at $6. Here it is: I am offering it to you right now for $6 a share. How much of it would you buy with your $2,400,000 in cash? How many shares would you be will-ing to buy right now at $6?"

He fidgeted around uncomfortably for a while and thought it over. "I'd say, maybe $100,000 of it."

"Then that's the amount you should own," I said. "Sell the rest today and leave yourself with $100,000 worth of this stock. *It's the same thing!* You would now own $100,000 of this stock and a little more than $2,300,000 in cash *after tax*! Sound good?"

He said, "I never thought of it that way. Neat trick. I'll have to think about that one."

Look at your current portfolio of investments. Would you buy them at their present valuations? Would you own as much of each investment as you do? If not, sell until your portfolio has both great diversification and many emotional hedges. You should not be excited or frightened to own what you own. And don't be afraid to pay the tax to get your portfolio diversified and emotionally balanced.

Six months later Joe's stock was selling for $1.20. He hadn't sold any of it.

And now, according to him, it was "too late."

I tried to tell him it was still worth $600,000 after tax. But he waved it off as chump change. "*I sold my entire business to them.* I'm not going to walk away with $600,000 at the end of the day."

He didn't—because four months later the stock was at 25 cents. Six months later the company declared bankruptcy. He never saw a dime of his tax-compounded money.

But here's the good news: In the end, he succeeded in not paying the government any tax.

CONTRARIAN VIEW OF THE FUTURE OF THE U.S. STOCK MARKET

The next time a stockbroker or investment professional tells you about the 10 percent a year theory, or that if you had invested in GE 40 years ago you'd be worth many millions of dollars, you may want to remind him or her that:

☞ Since the 1930s, the United States has gone from a country in major crisis, mired in a deep depression, about to enter into a world war, with an undeveloped stock market compared to the more established European markets, to becoming the biggest economy in the world, the biggest stock market in the world, and having a currency so strong it has overtaken gold as the world standard. The United States went from a country on the financial brink to the only superpower on earth!

☞ **That kind of exponential growth will not likely repeat itself over the next 70 years—or maybe ever! We would have to become virtually immortal as individuals and indestructible as a country for that kind of exponential growth in both safety and stature to occur again.**

Analyzing what has happened in the past can be a valuable tool. But attempting to look ahead is even more valuable. As the legal disclaimer in a fund's prospectus says: "Past performance is no guarantee of future results."

There is one fairly certain assumption about the future: There will be great bull market years ahead, as well as devastating bear market years.

With that in mind, even with traditional diversification methods (bonds included), statistics show that sustaining historically typical losses over the average bear market is too devastating for most investors to survive fiscally or psychologically.

I don't believe we should rely on future good times in the stock market to gain back devastating losses to our portfolios during bear market years.

Nor do I feel it's credible or prudent to rely on the 10 percent a year theory (or even the more realistic 5 percent a year theory).

During secular bear markets we cannot afford to ask ourselves to wait 10 to 20 years to prove that our 5 or 10 percent a year theory was ultimately repeatable.

HEDGE FUNDS: THE DARK SIDE

I explore the world of hedge funds in fuller detail later in the book (most specifically in Chapter 7), but on a purely factual basis, let's explore the dark side before getting carried away on a sea of "alternative investment" media hype.

Hedge funds by definition would have us assume that they are hedging us from risk. Most retail investors have only a vague idea of what hedge funds actually do to make money, or why hedge fund managers are able to charge fees that would be seen as obscene by those in the mutual fund industry. (Factually, hedge fund fees are far cheaper than mutual fund or brokerage fees in years they fail to make profits.)

Retail investors hear that hedge funds are hot, and they are for the superrich. Some of them blow up and go to zero, but others make big profits in bull markets and bear markets alike. And they wield enormous power over the financial markets and the companies whose stocks they invest in.

Many of these assumptions are not far from the truth, but of course the devil is in the details.

Successful hedge fund managers receive sizable salaries by making money for their investors even when the stock market is tanking. They promise an absolute return and don't mind betting against the stock market, leveraging investor assets, delving into all sorts of esoteric derivatives and options, or making money on high levels of volatility.

During the first few years of this century many hedge funds' returns soared past those of traditional investment portfolios, preserving principal during the bear market and making money during the recovery.

In *U.S. News & World Report* (according to the Opalesque alternative investment reporting agency, January 2, 2006), William Wechsler, a vice president with financial services consultants Greenwich Associates, pointed out that hedge funds have flourished in a protracted investment environment where investors were confronted with both low interest rates and sluggish equity markets.

Also according to *U.S. News & World Report*, the California Public Employees' Retirement System (CalPERS), the nation's largest pension plan, has about $1.2 billion invested in hedge funds and plans to nearly double that stake to increase.

University endowments, such as those of Yale and Harvard, and religious institutions, like the Roman Catholic Church, are also hedge fund investors.

There are about 8,000 hedge funds as of 2006. About 10 percent of them go out of business every year. Many hedge funds have lives of five years or less. And they are lightly regulated despite stricter Securities and Exchange Commission (SEC) laws put in place in 2006.

Still other hedge funds are fraudulent. Although frauds are statistically rare, you don't want to be victimized, even as a rarity. Therefore, institutional due diligence is critical before you choose any hedge fund for consideration.

This is from an article in the online alternative investment media service, Opalesque, from February 7, 2006:

> In a much applauded analysis presented at the 8th Alternative Investment Roundup in Scottsdale, Hunt Taylor gave examples how throughout history the media was actually creating fear. And in most cases, "what we are afraid of is not what we will die from." For example, after Chernobyl, CNN said about 3.2m people will die. The latest number Taylor could get about the fatalities of this Russian nuclear disaster [was] 4,000.
>
> Looking at press archives and publicly available records, Taylor . . . [summed up losses due to fraud] in relation to the total [hedge fund] industry . . . :
>
> Losses (B) as % of industry assets (A):

	A	B
2000:	$500bln	–0.11%
2001:	$563bln	–0.014%
2002:	$650bln	–0.18%
2003:	$817bln	–0.03%
2004:	$950bln	–0.00%
2005:	$1.1trln	–0.15%

> Even if you add up all hedge fund blowups since 2000, this would correspond to a 1% down day in GE, or –0.1% of the Dow Jones Industrial Average.

Nonetheless, fraud in the hedge fund world does happen, and without an extremely brilliant due diligence process, it could statistically happen *to you* far more frequently than to the average investor. (That is Murphy's law, not Taylor's.)

I would also presume that Taylor's analysis left out dozens of smaller frauds in the hedge fund world.

To be fair, there are frauds reported in all areas of the financial world: Financial advisers, advisory firms, private money managers of separately managed accounts, stockbrokers, and mutual fund firms and their managers, are all susceptible to fraud or theft.

But frauds in the hedge fund world are often headline makers, usually because of the high net worth of the investors involved.

HEDGE FUND AND MUTUAL FUND TAXES— BUYERS BEWARE

Hedge funds and funds of funds (limited partnerships in general) can have some very complex tax structures. Few of them are tax efficient simply because few strategies can succeed by simply buying and holding their investments. It is normal for a hedge fund, or fund of funds, to have a tax flow-through of 100 percent short-term gains or ordinary income. I find that acceptable if the trade-off for paying the taxes as you go offers *less risk and higher returns* than traditional investments over typical 5-to-10-year periods.

However, there are some extremely tax-inefficient strategies that can wreak havoc with your tax bottom line. You, your adviser, and/or your fund of funds manager must be held to the fire about doing proper tax analysis with any hedge fund manager you may be directly (or indirectly through a fund of funds) invested with. The question is, "What is the net (after all fees) *after-tax* performance of this investment?"

You may put individual retirement accounts (IRAs) into hedge funds through a custodial bank, but for now let's assume this is non-IRA money.

☞ Some funds cast off high amounts of expenses and fees that are not tax deductible to your bottom line on your K-1. (The K-1 is the form your CPA will receive from the fund at tax year-end.) Typically this occurs when, for various reasons, the fund must report expenses on Schedule A versus Schedule E (which most high-net-worth individuals then cannot deduct). You may still want to invest in such a fund, but calculate the after-tax performance first.

☞ Do any of the funds potentially incur high amounts of unrealized losses in a given year? These losses will not be deductible against the gains until the year they are sold and the losses are realized. Failure to redeem from the fund on December 31 or before can turn a positive performance year into a net *negative* after-tax event.

☞ The use of leverage can create tax events even for IRAs. If the fund or fund of funds uses leverage, always seek out information about how it may affect your IRA account.

☞ For offshore investors, be careful *not* to invest in U.S. trade or business strategies like asset-based lending or real estate. You will have to file a U.S. tax return and pay U.S. taxes.

The Positive Side of Hedge Fund Taxes versus Mutual Fund Taxes

Many mutual funds have unrealized gains hidden in their portfolios, so that when you take money out, or when one of your mutual funds sells those positions while you are still invested, massive amounts of *realized* gains (far beyond what you have personally gained in your account) may need to be reported on your taxes, leaving you with a potentially enormous tax burden. **These types of unfair "realized gains" tax flow-throughs rarely, if ever, occur with hedge fund investing.**

Many investors from 2000 to 2002 lost huge sums of money in their mutual funds and *also* ended up with outrageous tax bills.

But it can happen at other times as well. For instance, suppose you are invested in a mutual fund, and were even losing money in your account. If the fund then sells long-held stock positions that had made great profits for the fund *before you invested*, you would be held responsible for a percentage of the long- or short-term capital gains tax from the sale of the stock. In other words, you shared the tax burden of gains made before you invested! *This is still the law of the land.*

The same is true when a mutual fund reports a dividend

distribution. Even if you invested the day before, you will be responsible for paying tax on that income. Understand, your account made nothing from the distribution, since the net asset value (NAV) of the fund drops by an amount equal to the distribution. But you will still owe tax on the income that the distribution generated.

Hedge funds, by contrast, almost always tax each limited partner only on the share of the realized gains (or income) earned in his or her account. This is a far better tax deal than what you will receive in the mutual fund world, and it is a very big positive for hedge fund investing (or, more specifically, a big negative for mutual fund investing).

We must make a point of analyzing whether the gains in any strategy we invest in (including mutual funds and separately managed accounts) are worth the tax problems they may create.

Any fund that has a tax equivalent of 100 percent short-term gains or has 100 percent of its gains taxed as ordinary income is still worth your consideration *if* the risks to your assets are greatly reduced.

Check all other potential tax implications before you invest. You cannot judge the performance of an investment until you assess its net after-tax return.

Choosing a Hedge Fund

This is nothing you should ever attempt on your own. Institutional due diligence is critical to protect investors and to verify the accuracy of the fund's reported performance.

You must also take great care to assess the tax implications of the fund's performance as discussed in the previous section.

Beyond that, there is another problem: Inevitably the funds that most single investors become interested in are what we in the industry call "walk on water funds." Their returns annually are fantastic. The occasional monthly losses seem to be relatively tolerable. And the future seems bright—only because of the past.

Allow me to cite another example of an investor who became interested in putting some of his assets into a fund that had drawdowns (losses) as large as 25 percent over a multimonth period, but that was averaging over 30 percent net annually over a four-year period.

The problem with this kind of volatility is that Jake (not his real name) is looking backwards and seeing that it all came out well in the end. If it hadn't come out well each and every year, he would have pressed "Delete" and forgotten the fund's name long ago. But because it has performed well each year so far, he is enamored.

I can tell you—since studying statistics and doing quantitative as well as qualitative research is at the heart of what I do—that there is absolutely no guarantee statistically that the future will be as rosy as the past for that fund or any other fund. And since that fund is so volatile, the next big wind shear could crash the plane. That exact plane has held up during every wind shear it has encountered in the past. But that's the past. How many Challenger space shuttles had had the same problematic O-rings that failed on that shuttle? Why then did that shuttle break apart and not the previous shuttles? Investigators concluded that the unusually cold weather at launch played a part. But overall the past did not tell us enough about the future because the materials used on the shuttle and the conditions at the time were too volatile to predict a stable outcome.

You may look at this manager in question, for instance, and say he's too smart to crash. If he's down 25 percent you're going to add money to your account since statistically he should now recover rapidly. He has before.

However, there is no logical reason for him to recover. He doesn't have put options coming due, for example. If instead this time he makes a second huge mistake, he could be down 60 percent and in desperation make one final gamble that blows up the fund and sends it to zero.

Impossible, you say? The hedge fund world is littered with stories of great traders and famous managers, revered in the financial world, blowing up. Look at Long-Term Capital Management. (You may say LTCM was not an aggressive fund, or at least had never been volatile in the past. It had had no down months. It was averaging 40 percent a year! But that's my point. LTCM was 100 times leveraged! Therefore, the materials the plane was made out of were flawed even though returns had been great looking backwards and the plane had taken off and landed safely a thousand times.)

We should never, ever take a chance with a plane made out of that kind of volatile, unpredictable material, even though it has been flying for five years in all kinds of weather without crashing. The future is not ours to see. The only thing we can do is to assess quality and risk, not past performance. I have learned from experience that the only way to assess quality or risk is to understand the trading system and the volatility of that system under extreme stress, and do the math. (Or let someone else do the math.)

The studies I have done on aggressive investing versus conservative investing have amazed me: Aggressive investing always loses out to conservative investing during any fairly long time parameter. That's why I've given up on the concept of aggressive investing altogether. It's gambling pure and simple. Let's leave the gambling to the foolish and become rich instead.

Are Hedge Funds Worth Your Consideration?

My research has led me to the conclusion that there are not many good hedge funds out of the approximately 8,000 presently offered. Whether you're trying to choose a hedge fund on your own or are using an adviser or manager to choose the funds for you, the odds of continuous success for more than a five-year period in any single hedge fund are not good. In this light, buy and hold can seem like a bad idea for traditional investments and alternative investments as well.

Although it's true that some of the worst investments I have ever seen come clothed as hedge funds, it is also true that most of the very best investments I have come across in my career as an investment researcher are also hedge funds. It is an investment class with wild extremes in terms of quality, risk, reward, liquidity, fees, and safety.

The truth about investing—a truth that no adviser, analyst, broker, or media expert wants you to know—is that there is no magic bullet. And there is no way to know about future results over any length of time. The history of modern financial markets is too short to make any guarantees.

Diversification in and of itself is not a magic bullet, either. (Each piece of the diversification puzzle would have to act appropriately just when it is expected to in order to counterbalance other negative parts of the portfolio.)

The reason the future cannot be relied upon (past returns are no guarantee of future results) is that the inefficiencies and tendencies of the market, and the macroeconomic environment, are all constantly changing. And the ways they interact are constantly changing. We will *normally* see all sorts of things that have never happened before.

In the investing world, history rarely repeats itself, and, in fact, hardly ever rhymes (to paraphrase and contradict Mark Twain). When analyzing each market month they seem more like snowflakes than fingerprints—virtually nothing can be ascertained from previous flakes that will tell us with certainty about the exact design of the next flake. Life is about surprises. Profits come from being vigilant and moving with the momentum of a certain trend, whether it be gold or technology or value or bonds or real estate loans—until that trend ends and begins retracing itself or melting away.

(Continued)

Are Hedge Funds Worth Your Consideration? *(Continued)*

Hedge funds can be analyzed along a very similar model. You must know how to spot and move into winning strategies (or let a fund of funds manager attempt to do it for you).

If you can spot trends in the hedge fund industry and have institutional due diligence backing up your intuitive work, then it can be possible to create workable models with risk/reward parameters that often blow away the markets over a given market cycle.

The brighter side of hedge funds and other investment techniques is explored in Chapter 7, "Successful Investments: Where Are They?"

But for now, lesson one is: *Caveat emptor.*

5

Addressing Investors' Questions from Part One

Here are my responses to the some of the questions investors ask me most often.

What is the biggest challenge facing investors today?

The biggest challenge for investors is overconfidence—in the markets, in hedge funds, in their own ability to make informed decisions, in their friends' abilities to make informed decisions, and in the wisdom and honesty of the financial media, financial planners, brokers, and money managers. The list goes on and on. Most people do not understand the risks involved when they are investing their money, especially during a secular bear market. I believe the right way to invest is to have a hedge against any potentially devastating loss. Contrary to what most people believe, investing is not the time for any kind of risk taking, no matter how greedy the financial media makes you feel. Gold, oil, Google, real estate, shorting the U.S. dollar, all the present darlings of this day, will likely see the majority of people who invest in those things today lose money—not because the investments will necessarily lose money from their present prices, but because the very media that tempted the investors to "buy now" will taunt them to "sell now" when the lows of a midterm cycle come. That is just what fear and the media do. Then when they have gotten you to sell, some other so-called expert will come on TV talking about "buy and hold" and "buying the lows." So next time you buy and not sell at the lows, and it will turn out to be a WorldCom or an Enron. Most of the financial media is a wonderful comedy show for those with a sick sense of humor.

You sound a bit cynical. Is that cynicism part of being successful?

Actually, yes. I think successful investing starts with cynicism. When the cynicism is proven to be misplaced, it's replaced with skepticism and doubt. And after thorough due diligence, after you invest, there must be continuing inquiry and vigilance. But then again, I was born in New York. I'd listen to Mel Allen announce a Yankee game on the radio while I watched the game on TV. He'd scream that Bobby Richardson hit the ball to deep center and it was caught right at the wall, when I could see on TV he hit a pop fly to shallow center that the outfielder caught with one hand while spitting out a chew of tobacco. You tend to learn early when you live in New York.

What about opportunities lost because of *too much* skepticism?

I have come to see that great investors avoid the possibility of losing serious money in any single investment they make. Those who look back on opportunities lost, thinking, "I wish I had invested in that," are really just poisoning themselves with impossible expectations and setting themselves up to be sucker-punched someday. Those who actually *win* a risky bet only learn to believe what should never be believed—that risk wins. Taking on too much risk is a surefire way to set up your own financial ruin.

I want to stay focused on creating risk-averse profits for my family, friends, and clients. When you invest in a risky venture, unless you get very lucky, eventually you will lose way too much money, and emotionally the trauma you have to live with can be even more devastating than the loss of the money.

Some of the "darlings of the day" you mentioned a few minutes ago—gold, oil, real estate, and currencies—are often considered tools for diversification and hedging *against* risk.

As far as having them be a permanent part of your portfolio is concerned, the problem, as always, is massive volatility. If you are diversifying your assets to dampen overall volatility or even to generate profit in excess of, let's say, the S&P over a three-to-five-year period, things like gold and oil and real estate investment trusts (REITs) and biotech, or a great company like Google when you own it at more than $500 a share, could just as easily be destructive as helpful over that given three-to-five-year period. Even 5 percent positions in these kinds of things can ruin an entire year or more of your performance.

It's important to consider that investors, including the great ones, tend not to think in terms of decades. They have a shorter-term tolerance for underperformance than that. For instance, who kept gold as a 5 percent position in their portfolios during the 1990s? If that was a correct decision, when exactly should you have sold? And if you sold it, then it was not a diversification tool; it was a timing tool.

The average investor gets in their head to buy gold or whatever the TV expert is hawking that day, and they put gold back in their portfolio "permanently" (usually near a market top in that sector, since that is usually *why* the TV expert is talking about it). He or she was brought on the show because the public is suddenly clamoring for more information about these "easy profits." They will stay through the commercials to learn about how and why to buy, or not yet buy, this asset class they know nothing about, whose chart has begun to look parabolic.

As far as timing systems are concerned, I have checked out many timers all over the world, timing all sorts of things. So few managers can consistently make money from timing anything (at least since the end of mutual fund international arbitrage trades). But it becomes especially difficult timing things like metals, oil, any kind of commodities, currencies, or speculative stocks. I'm always skeptical when I hear about claims of success from timing any of these things. And of course back-tests aren't worth the paper they're written on.

What are some of the hidden investing pitfalls that most people never consider?

Next to overconfidence, which I mentioned earlier, the second biggest pitfall is greed, and therefore the tendency to take too much risk. Aggressive investments are very difficult to profit from over the short or long term.

I think another important factor that most investors fail to grasp is the devastating impact of losses: Make 100 percent and then lose 50 percent and you only break even. Lose 50 percent and you need to make 100 percent just to recover. Those are difficult hurdles to overcome.

Therefore, the key to success must then become protection of principal first and foremost. Knowing when to cut your losses, even with a hedge fund manager you respect, is life in the real world, where money is not just a number on a screen. Knowing when you will cash in your profits, or move away from a strategy that begins to falter, is of equal importance.

Most investors don't realize that they don't have to be aggressive to win.

In other words, they should look in the mirror and say to themselves, "*I don't have to spend my time worrying about a risky investment every day. I have a better life planned for myself than being held hostage to the movements of a volatile investment. My cautious investments will serve me well enough.*"

Instead, they hear tales of quick riches, or gambles that paid off for someone else, and they want to take a gamble, too. But almost all gamblers end up losing to the house. Time is on the side of the casino.

Everyone loves to win. And winning can be addictive. How do you work with people to help them with their addiction of going for the big win—the gambling mentality?

I had a mentor who told me the best thing that can happen to investors is to lose money on their first investments. Then they really get it in their bones that they are not invincible, not immune to failure. Then they learn to look for inherent dangers. They become more astute investors far sooner than the early winners do.

In fact, investing is about dealing well with failure, because failures occur constantly. It's the response to failure that separates the great investors from the poor ones. Gamblers respond poorly to both success and failure.

When things are going well, the gambler thinks: "Why quit now? I'm on a roll." When things are going badly they say: "I can't quit now, not until I make back what I've lost." But then if they are lucky enough to make back their losses, well, they're on a roll again! Why quit now? Their instinct was right after all. They are about to make a killing.

So at what point exactly does a gambler stop? Probably never. That's why they are gamblers in the first place.

A great investor knows, *"If this goes against me down to point X, I'm out. If I win up to point Y, I am going to book my winnings and move on to the next idea."* They know these things before they place their bet on a stock or sector, or an allocation model. That discipline helps them stay in the game.

The gambler will be done with the game only when all of his chips are gone. The final chips, of course, are placed in desperation: "Well, the only way to make back my money now is to take what's left and place it on one last great idea: red 7. The biotech company my friend told me about. Double or nothing."

Try playing double or nothing sometime by just playing a game of heads or tails. The game doesn't last very long no matter how many times in a row you may win. And most investment bets in the real world don't even give you a 50 percent chance of winning on the first try.

How does your career as a songwriter/singer/musician impact your financial advising and research?

I think there's a natural advantage or two that a musician can bring to the financial world: Playing an instrument professionally is all about complex pattern recognition. Songwriting and improvising are about thinking one step ahead of where you assume everyone else is expecting you to go. In a similar way, creating unique risk-averse ways to invest money in all sorts of volatile market environments has felt fairly natural to me—it feels like a very creative process. It's fun to find new approaches.

Other challenges that come up in the financial world are also similar to the music world: When you're improvising or performing onstage, everything is constantly changing in the present moment. You learn to think on your feet, occasionally under extraordinary pressure. I thrive on that for some reason. I have learned to do well with intensity and competition.

Also, as a songwriter my tendency is to want to think about things in a nonstandardized way. That's helpful, too, since thinking the way everyone else does rarely works in either world.

So this apparent occupational non sequitur really isn't.

If you could give an investor just one piece of advice, what would it be?

It would be: Don't play this investing game on your own unless you intend to do it 24/7. Investing is a zero-sum game. Therefore, be sober about who your competition is on the other side of every trade. Your competitors are usually institutional guys looking for a quick buck and a sucker to help them make it. You can't beat them a majority of the time.

Then there is always the possibility of being defrauded.

And there is the possibility of being hopelessly addicted to the investing game and having your life and time slip away almost unnoticed until it's too late. It's easy to find yourself kidnapped by greed and the need to win.

Bottom line: If you don't want to join them 24/7 with the intention of beating them at their own game, then the only way to win is not to play.

"Not to play" in this context means that you commit to creating a portfolio that hedges risk first and foremost. And never gamble any of your money away, even at the fringes of your portfolio.

6

The Right Stuff (and the Wrong Stuff)

VENTURE CAPITAL INVESTING: ZERO IN A MILLION

Once you have money, all sorts of interesting ideas seem to find you. One of my favorite radio financial advisers, Bob Brinker, calls the worst of these "shark attacks."

We all seem to be too smart to be ensnared by one, until it happens to us out of the blue. It is sometimes a cunning and sociopathically brilliant plan. Usually it's a plan that is designed to prey upon our desire for easy money.

Two of the silliest of these that I have run across are:

A foreign bank, which doesn't want to reveal its name, will pay you a guaranteed insured 5 percent a month. Here's all the paperwork to prove it, including the insurance policy guaranteeing no default. The minimum investment is $500,000. Wire it to this account in the Cayman Islands.

Or:

It's a legal fact that you do not have to pay your income tax. Just join our band of hotshot attorneys who will be suing the IRS sometime soon, and stop paying your income tax now. For an initial fee of $250 you, too, will be immune from paying taxes for the rest of your life.

In the case of venture capital investing, the business looking for financial backing can be a truly good idea created by good people with a real plan for success. The only problem is that the odds for success, no matter how confident and glitzy the marketing material may be, are extremely low. Let's say, for your sake, the odds are zero in a million.

Venture capital investing is in some ways the riskiest and most unpleasant way to lose money. The business plan usually describes a unique entrepreneurial enterprise. It seems like a good idea and a good business on the face of it. The entrepreneurs will often have gold-bordered brochures to support their very logical plan. They will list very smart investors who are backing it. They may invite you to meetings if they are local. They also usually have a very affable, smart man or woman who somehow becomes your personal confidant, an executive of the firm who gives you the inside scoop about what's going on and fills you in confidentially on whom they are talking to—Coca-Cola, Merck, Yahoo!, General Electric. This person craftily merges the business and its very logical plan with you and your money.

By the time you find out the lights are being turned off you have already become a believer in the gold-bordered brochure, and may have enjoyed hobnobbing with the CEO and CFO. You thought you knew what the CEO was really thinking, and knew all the secret things happening behind the scenes that were going to leapfrog this little company into the land of riches. Then the initial public offering (IPO) would increase your money 20-fold, and before long Microsoft would buy the venture.

But zero in a million are the odds that it will ever turn out the way we (and they) dreamed.

Statistically, the odds are actually better than that, of course. Perhaps they're 1 in 1,000 in a benign economic environment. I cannot find reliable statistics on this subject. But the key as an investor is to assume the odds are zero in a million. Because it will prevent you from dreaming that this time could be the time.

I had a client I'll call Fred, who had $5 million. I had devised a plan that would, if all the moderate assumptions came to pass, have him living comfortably on an annual basis while not touching his principal. But at the last minute another adviser persuaded him that since he could live off of $4.5 million using my same plan, he should take $500,000 and invest it in five different venture capital deals he had access to. This adviser felt the odds were high that at least two of the five would pay off, although there was no way to know which two. And even if only one of them paid off, Fred's $500,000 investment could double. If all five returned 10 times his money, he would have made *another* $5 million, doubling his present assets. This would take a few years. But there would likely be IPOs involved in at least a few of these investments and it could get "very exciting."

I explained to Fred that even if this came to pass it would not substantially change his financial life or his level of security from where it was now, and that he did not have to play these kinds of games anymore with his money. He had too much power to have to play with these kinds of risks.

I said, "Look in the mirror and tell yourself, 'I don't need to play these risky games anymore. I've already won. I'm done.'"

But he said that he had always wanted to be more involved in young entrepreneurial ventures. It was downright American to support young companies to grow and become great. He would personally check out each deal first to make sure that each one separately deserved his money. Then he would consider forcing himself to choose only the best two, instead of choosing five. That way he would be investing only $200,000.

After months of research Fred decided there were actually three start-ups that deserved his money, and that to "round off" the numbers he was going to give them $200,000 each.

This $600,000 became the focus of the next year of his life. He was far more interested in telling me about the progress of these three companies than he was delighted about the fact that our investments were doing well and were basically supporting his life. Turning his life into that of a venture capitalist, or investment voyeur, seemed to be a waste of his time in my eyes, but he certainly was excited every time we spoke.

Then came the sad news. One of the companies was going to have to shut its doors unless it got more funding. It was right at the cusp of great things. It had found a distributor and tons of buyer interest in Asia if only it could put together another $500,000 for the final push. It was willing to double the amount of preferred stock it would offer in return for anyone willing to invest. Then massive success was inevitable.

Fred had a long dinner with the CEO and the adviser who had introduced them, looked at spreadsheets and e-mails and letters exchanged between the company and "the top" Asian distributor, which was begging for product. Fred then came to me and asked for the money. I told him if he invested one dollar more of his money in this I would quit as his adviser. I told him if the deal was so good there would be plenty of willing investors. He already had too much at stake.

So he borrowed $150,000 from his credit line to help out the CEO, who had by now become "a friend and confidant."

Three months later, the lights went out. Not officially. Nothing ever officially came in the mail saying "We are done. We are broke. We failed. But thanks." The news just came in the form of unreturned phone calls.

Fred's other deals went similarly. All of them shut their doors within the year. Total losses were $750,000—15 percent of his net worth.

Don't assume you will see your money again when investing in a venture capital deal or fund.

Do not play with venture capital with the fringes of your portfolio, because if you do you will be in a no-win situation. The odds are that either you will invest so small a percentage of your net worth that even winning 20-fold will not noticeably change your financial life, or you will invest too much and lose big.

When you lose, it often negates too much of the conservative and steady types of gains inside the rest of your portfolio. If you win, you will almost certainly assume you can win again. And you will soon take that kind of risk again. To me that's a no-win situation.

Therefore, assume your chances for success with venture capital investments, along with their preferred stock, warrants, and the like, are zero in a million.

If you have already invested in a new venture, mark the position down to zero in your portfolio now. That means assume you will not ever see your money again. This is not a secure loan you can expect to have paid back. And the odds are not with you. Therefore, marking it to zero in your portfolio is the most prudent and realistic thing to do. If the outcome turns positive in the future it's like winning the lottery. But we cannot assume we will win the lottery.

The next time you're tempted by the latest get-rich-quick scheme a friend tells you about, ask yourself: "Do I want to be the CEO of a venture capital firm and make this my first investment?" If so, get your license and find clients. If not, then don't think you can tell the difference between a winner and a loser when all the other venture capital firms on earth, with all their staff and experience, are unable to tell winners from losers with any statistical consistency.

REAL ESTATE: LIVE IN IT.
THE REST IS INVESTING.

On the face of it, real estate is very alluring as an investment. It is often a great investment for the average person. I suggest everyone buy a home with their initial investable capital to get on a solid financial path.

First of all, the bank leverages your down payment. So if you put down $200,000 on a $1 million house and its value goes up by 50 percent over just three years (the kind of bubbly gain seen in many urban centers and retirement towns across the United States and Europe from 2003 to 2005), your $200,000 has increased to $700,000. That is a gain of 250 percent over three years.

To book that profit you would have to sell the property. Realtor fees when you sell, plus property tax, insurance, and repair costs, might bring the net gain down to around $380,000. (Realtor fees at 6 percent would equal $60,000 on a $1 million house. Property tax at, for instance, 1.5 percent on a $1 million house would be $45,000 over three years. Insurance would be another $5,000 over three years, and repairs perhaps another $10,000.)

Then there is the mortgage. But let's assume the mortgage minus the income tax deduction for interest paid was a neutral event since you would otherwise have had to rent.

All in all, this net 175 percent gain over three years looks like a brilliant investment.

And it was!

Why, then, would anyone ever bother investing in the bizarre and volatile stock market?

☞ Because this real estate example is the outcome of investing in an asset bubble, a once-in-a-lifetime event.

☞ Because the stock market's gains over time have dwarfed those of real estate.

☞ Because real estate can bankrupt you very quickly if things go wrong.

Let's go back to the real estate scenario. The leverage a bank affords you can work in reverse. The mortgage, taxes, and real estate agent fees at the time the property is sold do not go away.

If you put down the same $200,000 on a $1 million house and its value stays flat over three years:

Your $200,000 has remained the same. That is a gain of 0 percent. The cost of real estate fees when you sell, plus property tax, insurance, and repairs, might bring your net investment down to around negative $120,000. (As before, real estate fees would be $60,000 on a $1 million house. Property tax at 1.5 percent would be $45,000 over three years. Insurance would be another $5,000 over three years and repairs perhaps another $10,000.)

Let's assume the mortgage was a neutral event since you would otherwise have had to rent.

Your loss on the sale of the house would still be $120,000—60 percent of your down payment!

Ah, you say, but it's where you live. You simply won't sell it. You'll wait for the real estate market to grow skyward again and you'll be fine. Eventually you will make a lot of money.

☞ I do agree, if you can afford to stay in the house and wait out the downturn, and if you are not panicked into selling by roars from the financial media that the housing market is going to fall even further, and that your losses could become insurmountable if you don't sell now. Those are not easy issues to work around during a bona fide housing crash.

If you put down the same $200,000 for a $1 million house and it goes down in price over three years:

You put $200,000 down on a $1 million house, which you then sell for $800,000. After paying real estate fees and costs equaling about $108,000, using the same assumptions as in the previous examples, you cash out for about $692,000. But you still owe the bank $800,000 in mortgage. So your down payment is gone and you owe the bank *another* $108,000!

If none of that scares you away, I would say to have a nice life and enjoy your home. I am a big believer in owning real estate. At the very least, own the place you live in.

Just be careful not to overextend yourself and don't assume any gains in your equity over 5-to-10-year periods. In fact, do plan on what you might do if the market falls apart right after you buy your house. This is simply prudent fiscal management.

As far as *investing* in real estate is concerned, that becomes a more difficult game to win unless you find yourself in an asset bubble like the one we experienced in the late 1990s through 2005. Statistically it was a rarity, and will not likely come again for a very long time.

Own the house you live in. However, owning a second or third property as a rental property or an investment property is not something I recommend unless you are someone who will not stress out over bad tenants, lost monthly rent when tenants leave and you cannot re-rent it for a month or longer, lost monthly rent when the tenants don't pay you, the hassle of possible evictions, repairs on the house, property tax, property insurance, liability insurance, and being responsible for a second and third mortgage to a bank.

The bottom-line question is: *Is this the way you want to spend your time?*

TALE OF TWO BUBBLES

This seems to be a perfect time to examine *both* bubbles—the equity bubble and the real estate bubble—that we have all lived through:

Warren Buffett and Donald Trump have made billions of dollars. They invested early, kept investing even during the worst of times, suffered through massive losses, bought some more, and deserve the riches they have amassed. They have been true believers. They have outfoxed and outbid their competitors. Their methodology has had a long-term vision, and they could afford to continue playing and buying when the majority of players were being forced to sell.

But let's look at the facts from the average investor's perspective:

In the past 120 years, real estate has outperformed the stock market in only two out of the 12 decades: the 1930s, when both fell, but equities fell further; and the 1970s, which experienced a period of hyperinflation.

This decade, real estate was booming until it hit a wall in 2006. But could it recover in the coming year or two? Could this be the third decade out of the last 13 where real estate wins? It got off to a great start in the first half of the this decade. But a lot can happen in just a few years! Let's take a look.

San Francisco and Marin County

This was where I lived until we moved to Maui in 2000. The Bay Area real estate prices have trended upward over the past 20 years. This rise was interrupted only once by a severe commercial real estate recession, matching the U.S. recession in 1989–1991. Residential markets also suffered. I personally benefited from the mini-panic in 1989, as it afforded me my first house. I bought a house in Mill Valley for $389,000 that the previous owner had bought for $440,000. After real estate fees, he suffered a 15 percent loss over the five years he owned the house.

Many said this kind of depreciation could never happen in Marin County or San Francisco again. Then came 2006.

Los Angeles and California

Los Angeles real estate rose more than 25 percent just in 2004 (see Figure 6.1), and 2005 was another great year for property appreciation. But the past 25-year period was certainly a bumpy ride. The 1980s real estate boom came to a sobering end.

If you bought a house for about $250,000 in 1990 and it tracked the Office of Federal Housing Enterprise Oversight (OFHEO) index closely, by 1996 you would not have been able to sell it for more than about $200,000. **(This was a time when the stock market was soaring nearly 84 percent in the same six-year period.)**

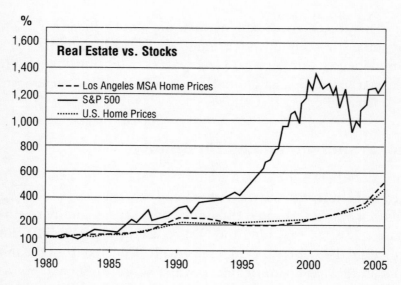

Figure 6.1   The stock market strongly outperforms the Los Angeles real estate market over the last 25 years.

Losses were far worse in higher-end markets. Some famous entertainers were caught in the Los Angeles downturn and were forced to sell their sprawling multimillion-dollar mansions in Beverly Hills at huge losses (if they could find a buyer).

New York City and New York State

New York City's real estate prices soared as high as the skyscrapers during the bubble years, which ended in 2005. (See Figure 6.2.) But at the end of the 1980s, a major real estate run-up was abruptly terminated by a rise in mortgage rates. **Home prices then gained less**

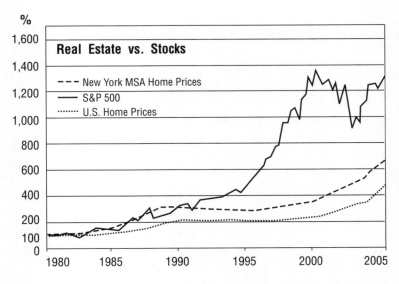

Figure 6.2 Although New York City's housing prices have strongly outperformed the national average since the mid–1980s, they still have fallen far short of the gains in the U.S. stock market during the same period.

than 2 percent a year from late 1989 to early 1999 while the stock market exploded.

Interestingly, during the same bubble period, while parts of Long Island saw dramatic price increases, upstate New York saw hardly any appreciation at all.

You can still buy a modern five-bedroom, 4,000-square-foot house in the beautiful rolling, forested hills near Pittsford, New York, where I have spent some time in the summer months, about 20 minutes from the city of Rochester, for about $400,000.

This is because employment, and therefore demographic growth in the area, is not increasing. Rochester's two main corporations—Xerox and Eastman Kodak—were cutting jobs during the housing bubble years. The rest of the area's smaller companies, and its emerging technology sector, could not take up the slack.

Miami and Florida

In the 1920s Miami's real estate was in an incredible bubble. People saw Miami as a glamorous city and rushed in to buy "before land ran out," only to suffer from the crash of the 1930s. It took real estate in Miami decades to recover.

In the 1960s, Miami and many other parts of Florida exploded during the "condo boom." But the end of that boom, which occurred in the early 1970s, came when condominiums crowded every market in every town in the state. Thousands of developers and their REIT investors quickly went broke as inflation and interest rates rose far faster than the flooded housing market. **(This boom ended while inflation was rising—inflation hit 13.5 percent in 1983—and the stock market was steadily profiting.)** (See Figure 6.3.)

According to a report by Raymond James & Associates, investment and speculation accounted for as much as 85 percent of condo sales in downtown Miami by the end of 2005!

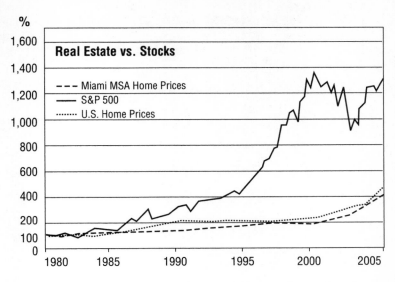

Figure 6.3   In Miami, no one talked about real estate being the place to put all your investment dollars versus the U.S. stock market—until after 2000.

Conclusions

Even during real estate bubbles, certain criteria must be met for prices to rise dramatically in a given area:

☞ There are strong employment opportunities, and/or there is a vibrant university economy.

☞ There are increases in population, and therefore there is increasing demand for housing.

☞ The area is considered a warm and wonderful place to retire.

Prudence suggests that even the real estate markets meeting these criteria will have long periods of underperformance versus the equity markets, and that both asset classes will spend plenty of time on the dark side of the moon.

During most decades equities will outperform real estate if the past 100 years are any indication.

THE VIEW FROM A FAMILY OFFICE

A family office is an office dedicated to the investments of a multigenerational family: a family possessing enough money to invest for themselves, their children, and their grandchildren. It typically costs $1 million or more annually just to run such an office, with hired advisers and so forth. Therefore, a family office would generally be managing at least $100 million in assets for it to be worth their while. The family net worth is often 5 to 10 times that.

At an absolute returns conference in Bermuda in April of 2000, I met the chief adviser to a family office. The family's name could not be disclosed; nonetheless, two very important observations were made by this very smart professional.

Only 3 to 5 Percent Maximum in the Stock Market

I asked this adviser to the superrich what percentage of the family office's assets were invested in the stock market.

He answered, "I would say 3 to 5 percent is invested directly in the market without a hedge. But that would be for the accounts of children a generation or two out. We would not, in general, want to risk investing directionally for anyone presently living."

Why? Because when you have that much money, neither the risk nor the volatility of the stock market is worth the gamble. Not now. Not ever. These people are at the End Game. They no longer have to play, and wouldn't think of it!

So what do you invest in when you have that much money?

His answer: "Baskets of extremely conservative hedge funds, hedged accounts, and real estate bought and overseen by a development corporation that the family owns. Again, we are not so much betting that the price of real estate will increase—we are slowly developing raw land that has already been permit approved."

The Start of a Bull Market

The adviser then relayed a very interesting story to me.

He had been the chief financial adviser to a huge oil conglomerate in the late 1970s and early 1980s before taking his present job. He went to the board of directors in 1980 and said he thought the U.S. stock market was undervalued and suggested they put 10 percent of their free cash in a large basket of U.S. stocks.

"Let's invest 10 percent of our cash in the U.S. stock market."

And the board said, "Why the heck would we throw our money into a toilet bowl?"

There were no buy-and-holders in the room!

They had just lived through the 1970s. Their view of the stock market was that it was volatile, likely to lose 25 to 40 percent at any time, and was obviously incapable of keeping up with inflation.

The stock market was dead. It would never recover. Inflation would never be completely tamed. The government was in chaos. Companies were floundering. And so on.

Of course, *this is what the beginning of a bull market often looks like!*

Upon Reflection

The view of the day is merely a reflection of the recent past. It is very difficult for people to make money when they assume that "what is" today will remain the same tomorrow.

PS: It is even harder to make money when people assume they know how and when things will change!

I have yet to meet the astrologer, soothsayer, market timer, gold bug, or oil magnate who can predict with 100 percent accuracy the ups and downs and shifts in the marketplace.

Recessions: How to Define, and Stay Out of the Way of, a Ghost

A recession is really more like a ghost than a hurricane: appearing and disappearing through time, hard to pin down, and virtually impossible to predict.

In fact, like a ghost, it could turn out to be more like Casper the Friendly Ghost (a refreshing scare that resets the economy or the markets), or it could wreak serious havoc on the economy and the markets, vaporizing jobs, housing and equity valuations, and tax revenue earmarked for the government's precious budgets and other political boondoggles.

Some define a recession as two straight negative quarters of gross domestic product (GDP). The National Bureau of Economic Research created a more specific definition of recessions that takes into account three dimensions of the decline in aggregate economic activity—its depth, duration, and diffusion across industries (the three Ds).

One thing we all know is that before a recession comes to pass the markets get wind of a reversal of economic growth, and that is the time of the worst and most volatile stock market performances.

How can you avoid these declining and volatile periods as a traditional investor? In all likelihood you can't. How can you stay out of the way of a ghost, something that you can't see? A recession is typically defined only after it is already upon us, or has already come and gone.

History shows that the stock market is often falsely alarmed—so even timing out of the market when the market or the media is *predicting* a recession does not work. As economist Paul Samuelson humorously noted:

"Economists have correctly predicted nine of the last five recessions."

Stock markets have a similar track record of reacting to false information.

When a financial planner or stockbroker tells you that the answer instead is to simply buy and hold, and that the U.S. stock market has averaged a 10 percent annual return since 1940, Chapter 4 gives you plenty of ammunition to debate these professionals. But most likely they will only throw statistics back at you to refute your claim and the debate will never end.

The *undebatable* question we then come to is this:

How might I avoid the massive volatility and heavy losses that are caused by recessions and the breaking of speculative bubbles?

I believe hedging your portfolio is the answer.

Tax compounding when factored in weighs on the side of buy and hold. But the fiscal devastation and emotional challenges of holding on during down periods make that method of investing too costly and emotionally unreasonable versus other very profitable and less volatile ways of investing, such as hedged funds of funds.

Ghostbusters

Proper hedging is critical for any investor who does not have a multi-decade investment horizon and a great tolerance for volatility.

One note of caution for those brave souls who *do* have a multi-decade investment horizon and think they are capable of handling huge losses in their accounts along the way:

You must also have a tremendous faith that history will repeat itself.

The "10 percent a year" statistic is backwards-looking.

My logic says: we *cannot afford* to rely on the assumption that the United States and its corporations will ever repeat the exponential growth and maturation they have experienced since the end of World War II.

WHAT DOES THE FED REALLY WANT?

Everyone talks about the Federal Reserve, and whether it is going to raise or lower interest rates or stay on the sidelines. Many believe these rates have an effect on the economy six to nine months out. Some very credible economists, like Dr. John Hussman, do not believe the Fed has that much control over the long-term direction of the economy regardless of how it moves rates. They believe the economy and inflation are controlled more specifically by the levels of the current account and trade deficits.

But without question, for the individual or small business owner, rates matter. For instance, rate hikes can make mortgages unaffordable. They can make loans to small businesses uneconomical.

So almost as a monthly ritual, every investor asks, "What will the Fed do?"

To even have a clue about what it will do we need to ask, "What does the Fed really want?"

The answer is not entirely obvious. The Fed does not just aim for a scenario where there is zero inflation. It wants some amount of inflation. The Fed wants the economy, real estate, and the stock and bond markets to have the look and feel of normalcy—no bubbles, and conversely, no extraordinary weak spots that could eventually move us into a depression some years down the road. That is clearly the goal of any Fed for the long term: steady, calm growth (2 to 3 percent annually), with mild inflation (1.5 to 2.5 percent annually), for instance.

Therefore, mild inflation is actually good. (Price deflation can lead to depression.)

Most of what the Fed does is based on guesswork, because:

We are typically roaming about in The Great Poppy Fields of Unknown Statistical Information (not the stuff song titles, or easy profits, are made of).

Recurring Economic Cycles

Here is a thumbnail sketch, in general terms from the worst to the best, of nine economic cycles:

1. Global depression—In the United States, along with most of the world, during the 1930s.
2. Runaway inflation—As in Germany after World War I, before World War II.
3. Mild depression—As in Japan in the 1990s.
4. Stagflation—Recession plus inflation, as in the United States in the mid-1970s.
5. High inflation—As in the United States in the early and late 1970s.
6. Recession—Most recently in the United States in 2000–2002.
7. Mild recession—Most recently in 1989–1990.
8. Mild inflation—Most recently in the United States in 1999 and 2003–2006.
9. Inflation neutral—Goldilocks economy: "Not too hot, not too cold," as in 1995–1998.

Note: Cycles 1 to 4 have been bad periods for stock markets. Cycles 8 and 9 have been good or great for stock markets. The effects on the stock market regarding the rest of the cycles are dependent on a multitude of other factors. It is also rare to know with certainty exactly which cycle we are in at any given time.

Therefore, it is not often that any fail-safe predictions can be made about market direction. (See earlier statement about the Poppy Fields.)

THE DIARY OF AN INTUITIVE INVESTOR

Let's set the record straight right from the beginning. The term *intuitive investor* is just another name for *gambler*, because without deep knowledge, a strict methodology, and stop-losses in place, winning over the long term is very, very difficult to do, even for an investor with great instincts.

Sometimes gambling in the markets works for a while—especially if the market overall is roaring forward. However, when intuitive investing works but does not work *consistently*, that is called "playing chicken with a freight train" or "winning the battle and losing the war." But I digress.

Let us begin at the end, where this person's story began: It was Kyle's retirement party. He had saved $240,000, was 65 years old, with a wife, two kids in high school, and the perfunctory Irish setter that he never quite fell in love with (this was the same dog the kids would bequeath to him and his wife when they went off to college).

The night of his retirement party was fateful indeed, because a friend of his told him about this amazing money manager who could pick stocks like nobody's business. These were not stocks like GE and Intel and Microsoft where "anyone can make money." These were unknown, undervalued companies. Some of them were penny stocks. These were the rising stars.

Kyle had invested money in the stock market through his 401(k) plan and his wife's IRAs. They had done quite well, which he vaguely assumed was at least in part merely lucky timing during the 1990s bull market. Yet Kyle also felt he had made some pretty astute moves along the way. In fact, looking back, he had had a very good intuition about stocks and investing, but had never really pulled the trigger or trusted his instincts the way the big players do. He wondered what might have happened to his portfolio if he had been allowed to make use of his analytical abilities (he was an electrical engineer, a designer, and a part-time inventor).

A few days later he met this exceptional money manager his friend told him about in a café. He liked him very much. The manager said that he could invest early in these young companies and make a killing as each of them fulfilled its great promise. It was stressed that these were public companies, not venture capital start-ups. Kyle was skeptical at first. He asked a hundred questions about the companies: what they did, how many employees they had, what the growth rate and financial health of each company looked like. He asked why this manager thought they were undervalued. And in the end he asked how many other investors this manager had, and if the manager himself had invested his own money in these companies. And how much?

Kyle was quite proud of his due diligence, but needed even more information. He was sent beautiful packages on each prospective company. He read all the details. The information got very specific. They had products and great plans. He read for hours and days on end until finally he was ready to buy some stock.

The problem was that there was a minimum of $250,000 per portfolio for new clients. This assured proper diversification, the manager explained.

Kyle certainly was not about to take his entire life savings and risk it on these companies. But after a number of conversations he talked the manager down to a $125,000—half of his life savings. Diversification would still be there because he would also invest in larger-capitalization mutual funds outside of this manager's account, just like he did in his 401(k) plan. And the manager assured him of diversification in his portfolio as well. Some fringe ideas would have to be omitted, but he would make sure a sector balance was there. Fair enough.

The initial six-month period got pretty scary. Kyle was down over 15 percent at one point. He regretted buying these stocks at times. But he called the manager often and followed events almost daily. The manager assured him all was well and that patience was the key.

Then the news came: Three of his stocks had a great run during the beginning of 1999. Kyle was up over 20 percent since he invested just eight months earlier. He quickly realized he was annualizing at 30 percent. The manager said, "*This* is how millionaires make their money." Kyle got excited and put in another $50,000 by liquidating some of his large-cap funds, which had gone nowhere.

As it turned out, 1999 was a great year for Kyle. He was up over

60 percent for the year. He was well on his way to becoming a millionaire. He made another 15 percent in February of 2000 alone! He was stunned and giddy. The manager was a demigod for he had just about doubled Kyle's original money in a very short time.

Kyle celebrated with his wife, who had been very skeptical in the beginning and quite upset at the perceived risk he took with half of their retirement money. She asked him to sell half of the stocks the next day and put the originally invested money back in the bank. He said that first of all he could not sell yet because of capital gains rules. There would be too much tax to pay. But second, there were still great opportunities to take advantage of. He assured her he was following the companies almost every day and getting research papers in the mail constantly. It wasn't like he was a normal investor. He knew these companies. He was on top of it. His instincts were fine-tuned about these things now, especially after all he had learned last year about being patient during the initial 15 percent fall. He trusted the manager, who was brilliant. They were like brothers in arms. He gently chided his wife about her being upset when he canceled their vacation the year before because he was going to an important investor meeting one of his companies had sponsored, and now she admitted it all seemed worth the time and effort. She was proud of him, really. Vacations could wait. Now they could afford good colleges for their two children. They had assumed both their son and their daughter would have to go to state schools to save money. But now the son could follow his dream and see if he could get into Stanford University. And the daughter might get into Yale. They were very proud to be able to support their brilliant children's dreams and get them off to a great start in life.

The next six months were frightening. The stock market became extremely volatile. Some days when the indexes fell hard his stocks held on, but by October 2000 he had lost 30 percent. His original $125,000 plus his added $50,000 had turned into approximately $285,000 but had now fallen back to $200,000. His large-cap mutual funds were also doing badly since he had stayed invested in only his previous best performing funds (which he now realized owned a lot of big tech stocks). They were well on their way to losing half their value from their peak. So he was down almost 30 percent in those funds as well.

The Internet bubble had been pierced. And somehow, without quite realizing how it happened, he was waist deep in the fallout.

He began reading over some of his original notes on this manager. The notes said over and over again that these stocks were going to be "value stocks."

Value was outperforming growth in 2000. But his manager's stocks were apparently not value stocks at all. Maybe they had been long ago, but they were hardly that anymore. The manager thought it was important to be tax efficient and never sold his winners. But that made no sense, because his value portfolio had turned into a growth portfolio. Now he was taking massive losses, with tax efficiency as the excuse for why he was holding on.

Kyle watched CNBC all day long now, and would watch some of his stocks rolling by on the bottom of the screen every hour or so, down another $2, or down $6 on a bad market day. Those were days of hell. Even though he thought the companies were still filled with potential he felt strongly he should sell out.

His idea was to seek out new, younger companies and use his instincts and phenomenal entrepreneurial prowess to pick the next great winners while they were still in their infancy. Why should he pay his manager fees when he saw danger coming before the manager did?

Finally, not wanting to get literally ill watching thousands of dollars slip away in a single day, Kyle sold his stocks, in essence firing the manager. He was approximately at breakeven by the end of this 20-month journey. Plus his accountant said he owed taxes on the sale of his portfolio of mutual funds. But there was no time to look back. He had a new plan.

He spent Christmas of 2000 locked away in his makeshift office in the attic. His children never even had a chance to speak with him. They were teenagers and pretended not to care, but his wife was not pleased. They needed a father now more than ever.

However, he was in crisis mode and was feeling shame and a great sense of having let the family down. Stanford and Yale were out of the question at the moment. But he was determined to rectify that before it was too late. Staying in cash was a dangerous thing. The markets had rallied back a bit and his investment money was on the sidelines. It was all extremely upsetting. What made it worse was that his family just didn't understand, and offered very little support unless he was winning big.

According to research he read (research that had previously been right about the 2000 bear market, and called the tech bubble almost to the month) Kyle was convinced that Japan was ready to pull out of its deep recession and that the markets there would make money even as the U.S. markets continued to decline. He read other research, some that agreed with this theory and some that did not. But he felt strongly the oncoming bull market in Japan was going to be a gold mine for those who got in early. He invested all of his money in several diversified sectors and capitalization sizes of Japanese mutual funds offered at Charles Schwab.

Eight months later Kyle realized that the Japan theory was not correct. He sold his Japanese funds at a further loss. He also owed more tax from some of the mutual funds he lost money in. This seemed so unfair: another screwup in the tax laws.

After taxes and the Japan failure he was underwater compared to day 1, but not as badly as index investors were. That was his only solace.

He searched for lessons learned. One lesson was obvious: It felt a lot better to have money for his two children's college educations than not. The older one was at this moment up in his room applying to Stanford. The value of his house had increased nicely. He could always take out a second mortgage.

But the other lesson, upon reflection, was that he still trusted his instincts as an investor. Kyle decided not to listen to anyone else anymore—not newsletter writers, not TV analysts—and to do research on his own. Research was what made him a successful engineer and inventor. He felt he could apply the same abilities to the stock market as long as the experts on TV weren't yammering away at him and constantly pulling his emotions in two opposing directions.

It was the end of 2001. He looked at the enormous losses in the indexes over the past two years, including those from 9/11, and reminded himself again that he was in some way talented to have nearly broken even when all of his friends' 401(k) plans were now down 20 to 30 percent.

Kyle felt the market was ripe for a recovery. The feeling in the country was that of extreme patriotism and optimism. All the bad news was out. The terrorists were on the run in Afghanistan. He could smell a rally coming, but he wanted to be smart about it. There was no way he was going to buy tech stocks. He researched what sectors did well coming out of a recession, but not aggressive sectors that could lose 20 percent in a week. Could there be a calmer, saner way to make good, steady profits and lower the daily volatility?

He found the answer: high-yield bonds (junk bonds). These bonds were depressed from two years of strong declines. If there was even a perception of an economic recovery, high-yield bonds could be up 20 to 30 percent in a year, whereas if he was wrong, high-yield after two bad years had rarely ever had a third bad year, and when it did it was only a moderately bad one. He would also be accumulating very nice income from the bond yields. This was the conservative approach he had been searching for. So he researched the best high-yield bond funds and placed his bets cautiously over a two-month period.

Then Enron happened. Then Tyco. The markets swooned, and high-yield bond funds took massive losses. Kyle kept waiting impatiently for the bottom to come. But every week brought more bad news about U.S. companies, large and small, whose books were apparently rigged.

He began to believe from all these stories on TV (he began watching it again) that most companies were cooking the books one way or another. Some techniques were probably illegal, while some were barely legal. They were all a bunch of thieves really.

Slowly it occurred to Kyle that what many experts were now saying was right—this was the tip of the iceberg. U.S. stocks were still massively overvalued in reality. He was in shock from being down 20 percent for the year, but there was still time to be a hero and get on the winning side of the game.

He read everything he could get his hands on about the markets. He read the news. It was bad. He talked about politics with his friends. Everyone was beginning to have a sinking feeling about the Iraq war.

Finally, in October of 2002, Kyle took a shot and shorted the S&P 500 index (betting the market would continue to fall). The situation in Iraq was becoming a quagmire many equated with the Vietnam War. The federal budget, which a few short years ago showed massive surpluses, now had an all-time record deficit. He saw the writing on the wall. The country was going to suffer great political and financial losses, and the books of the companies were cooked. We might even go into a depression.

Unfortunately, that S&P short was placed pretty much at the bottom of a cyclical bear market. Markets always look and feel like that at the bottom—doom and gloom are everywhere. And as 2003 unfolded, a sharp and very serious rally got under way.

At first the rally came in fits and starts. But by May the market took off and never looked back. He lost another 15 percent of his life savings before he finally pulled out, realizing for the first time that he did not know any more than his friends and neighbors did about the markets, even with all the research he had done. His instincts were not only unreliable; they were in many ways counterintuitive, but not with enough consistency to profit by betting against his own instincts. So basically *everything* was *random*. And he was too often on the wrong side of random.

Kyle went into a bit of a depression for the first time in his life. He remembered a line from a movie—*The Cider House Rules*: "Whether or not I will be the hero of my own life, I do not yet know." He began to consider he might die a failure.

His life savings were now down to $170,000 from $250,000—a loss (not including the taxes he had to pay on his 1999 gains) of 32 percent.

He had to take out more money against the equity in his house to pay for living expenses.

The lessons Kyle had learned were:

Never trust research, experts, newsletters, or anyone talking about the stock market. Never trust companies and how they do their accounting.

The conclusion his instincts were now telling him was: Never invest in the market again. He took his remaining $170,000 and put it in U.S. Treasury bills as the market continued to climb, and his stomach continued to churn.

In 2005, seven years after his retirement, Kyle at the age 72 contemplated going back to work part-time. There were bills to pay. The children were both in state colleges—it was all the family could afford—but even they were far more expensive than he had assumed they would be. And the equity in their home, even though the value had increased dramatically, was now just about tapped out from his cash-out refinancing.

His next intuition in late 2005 told him to buy more real estate. Thankfully, he couldn't get a second loan.

More lessons learned:

☞ Take vacations when they are planned—they may not come around again.
☞ Trust your instincts only at your own risk.

Analysis from a Jester's Viewpoint

Jesters were quite valuable to kings all over Europe for centuries. That was because through humor they could tell the king to his face what few others could say in a sober manner without putting their very lives in jeopardy. So let's take a jester's view of lessons learned from the story of Kyle, because sometimes if you don't laugh, you just have to cry.

A THEORY STEPHEN HAWKING HAS YET TO DISCOVER: PARALLEL INVESTMENT UNIVERSES

It is apparent to any professional in my business that the market loves to win at everyone else's expense. The percentage of winning investors throughout a full bull and bear market cycle is extraordinarily low for such a popular and highly touted game. The only two ways to win seem to be either to invest in a diversified way in a secular bull market trend for 10 to 20 years, or to play the game "the right way." (More about that in the next section.)

For all the others—those who think they might be able to beat the system over time—the rule of parallel investment universes seems to apply. It goes like this:

Let's say on a given day you think the market is going to go up and I think the market is going to go down.

You put all your money into the market, and I at the same time take all my money out.

The theory of parallel investment universes says: For you the market will crash. For me it will have a spectacular rally.

That is because the market is an amazing equalizer—it scoops up losing bets like a multidirectional vacuum cleaner. In the end, the market is the only one that seems to come out winning.

On a slightly less cynical note: Investors during the great 1982–1999 bull market averaged gains of only about 3 percent a year while at the same time the market was annualizing at about 14 percent. How can that be?

The only answer I can think of is that there are parallel investment universes where multiple investors betting on hundreds of different hunches were all losing at the same time. After all, Warren

Buffett, George Soros, and Julian Robertson were not making the rest of the money all by themselves. Or were they?

Here's another intriguing question: Where does all that money go when a market crashes?

If a stock or real estate market loses 40 percent, is someone making 40 percent on the other side of the bet?

No!

That 40 percent goes to what they call "money heaven." It just disappears from the face of the earth.

If someone values your house at a million dollars, but a year later the only buyer in sight is willing to pay a maximum of $600,000, and you sell it, where did the $400,000 go?

The buyer did not make it, because no one else will buy it *from him* for a million dollars, either.

It just disappeared into the sky. It was a phantom gain. And it then turned into a phantom loss!

The lesson here—this is the last time I'll say it—is: *Do not try to outsmart the market*. Betting against the casino is not going to be a winning strategy over the long run.

What are your other options?

There is really only one option when it comes right down to it: If you want to win not just a few battles, but the war itself—you have to do the right thing *all the time*.

INVESTMENT GODS SAY: "DO THE RIGHT THING"

The question that begs to be answered is: What is the right thing? The right thing is an overall investing mind-set that includes the following beliefs:

- ☞ Always diversify.
- ☞ Always hedge.

☞ Do not take undue risks in any one investment, not even at the fringes of your portfolio.

☞ Assume that everything you assume is going to be wrong with great regularity.

☞ Don't listen to friends' investing ideas or to schemes that are too good to be true.

To continue with my jester's assessment of the financial world, there are deities in the investment world, much like the Greek gods of old.

These gods watch everyone placing their market bets. They love to punish wrongdoers and reward those who do right, but they like to string them both along to teach them lessons that will last them at least one lifetime, maybe more.

For instance, they may let speculators win a few battles until they are cocky enough to bet their entire life savings on their apparently fantastic market instincts. Then *wham*, the gods wipe them out in one fell swoop. Ah, they never tire of watching poor fellows squirm.

However, when they see investors taking a more diversified and cautious approach, and when they see these same investors bowing in fear to the market deities by hedging every bet they take, then even though the gods might make these investors squirm at first—perhaps by having them break even while the market makes 20 percent in six months, just to test their resolve—the gods eventually respect these investors' persistence and quiet courage. They respect when these investors continue to hedge their risk even when they are winning—refusing to try to parlay those winnings into a quick fortune. They watch as these investors turn down supposed no-fail opportunities every time. The gods feel respected. Eventually the gods make sure these investors are rewarded handsomely over the course of their lives.

From a jester's viewpoint, this is the way of the world.

I would be happy to let these jesters teach my children about investing, rather than letting them listen to some "clown" in the financial media talking about the latest hot tip. I'd be happy to let the jester teach my children rather than subjecting them to this year's top financial newsletter writer. In the long run, the jester's wisdom will win out.

Now, let's assess what "doing the right thing" looks like in far more detail.

Part Three

HEDGING WALL STREET: HEDGED PORTFOLIO CONSTRUCTION

7

Successful Investments: Where Are They?

Putting Together a Portfolio

ARE YOU A CONSERVATIVE INVESTOR OR AN AGGRESSIVE INVESTOR? OH, SHUT UP.

How many financial planners and advisers have you heard this from, except for the "shut up" part?

Well, let me tell you what you are, because I already know:

If you've been making money, or believe you are about to make money because everyone else has lately, then you want to be an aggressive investor. You are completely open to taking risks and making a lot of money. You can hang in there during the bad times.

If you've been losing money, then you want to be a conservative investor. You have lost your faith in the markets, and losing money is definitely not something you want to have happen again anytime soon. Let's not take any chances.

All you have to do now is know beforehand what will occur!

The real answer to the question is specific to the individual and/or his or her family *circumstances*, but should not be based on an investor's *emotions*, whims, or tolerance for gambling.

I tell my clients that I would like to decide whether they should be aggressive or conservative in their investing, rather than them telling me which they want to be, because that never works. In fact, it almost ensures failure.

As a general rule, as you approach or surpass the level of qualified investor ($1.5 million) conservation of principal is overwhelmingly more important than growth for reasons explained in the previous chapters.

Now let's get to your portfolio.

THUMBNAIL SKETCH OF PRUDENT PORTFOLIO CONSTRUCTION

Everything Is One Portfolio

The first thing I suggest to set up the template for successful investing is to consider all of your assets and debts as one big portfolio.

It's as Simple as 1, 2, 3, . . . 4

1. **No debts.** Without a doubt, the first thing to do is pay off all credit card debt. Next, pay down your home equity credit line. Then repay all bank and personal loans. There is no way anyone should be "investing" money they don't own.

   The only exceptions to this rule are debts from car loans or leases and/or mortgages, since one would assume the underlying assets are worth more than the debt.

   What you have left is excess liquidity.

2. **Accessible cash.** It is important to always maintain a cash position to cover at least three months of expenses plus an emergency cushion. Emergencies may amount to anywhere

between $25,000 to $50,000, depending on your situation, and the number of family members you have.

3. **Buy a house.** If you have not done so already, your first investment should be in a house you want to live in. But don't look at it as just an investment. It's where you live. When all is said and done, it is in many ways your most important investment.

4. **Calculate your remaining liquid net worth, and invest it.** Let's say you have $100,000 in liquid capital left over that does not seem to be needed for the next few years. This is investable capital.

When Looking at an Investment Portfolio: Think in Percentages, Not Dollar Bills

As your assets grow, sometimes even the slightest shift in your portfolio can amount to a large movement of dollars up or down. That is why right from the start of my investing career I learned to think in percentages, not dollar bills.

For instance, if you have a portfolio worth $10 million and it drops in value by 1 percent, you might panic at the thought that you just lost $100,000!

Or if you invest $2 million (20 percent of your assets) in a conservative hedged fund of funds with 20 managers in it, at first you may feel that putting $2 million into one investment is too risky. But if you break it down and realize that 20 percent of your assets are invested in a conservative hedged format with the average allocation to each manager equaling 1 percent of your personal net worth, you may come up with a different, more comforting conclusion.

Investing is about percentages. We need to analyze our true percentage risk versus our after-tax, after-inflation percentage reward with every investment we make.

No one should be trying to coerce us into investing our money. We may be well served having virtually all of it sitting in laddered Treasury bills and Treasury inflation protected securities (TIPS).

From that very risk-free after-tax return, we then must assess what risk we are willing to take for a potential return *above* that Treasury bill or TIPS rate.

Assessing these things by thinking in dollar bills is a far more difficult and often misleading exercise.

We will now look at two theoretical portfolios that may very well be worth the risk.

PORTFOLIO 1: FOR FUTURE MILLIONAIRES— DIVERSIFICATION AND DOLLAR COST AVERAGING

If you are not a qualified investor—someone with a net worth of $1.5 million including the equity in your house and both spouses' incomes—you need to look at alternatives to hedge funds and other types of limited partnerships since the law at present does not consider you a "sophisticated investor," whereas if you do have $1.5 million, suddenly you are a sophisticated investor. Ah, the wit and wisdom of the U.S. government. But I digress.

The first thing I think about when advising nonqualified investors, considering the overall quality and added value of stockbrokers, financial planning firms, and mutual fund firms, is this quote from the playwright Jane Wagner:

> *No matter how cynical you get, it's impossible to keep up.*
> —Jane Wagner, from *Crazy Wisdom*
> by Wes Nisker (Ten Speed Press, 1990)

Let's explore the "Jane Wagner" side of the equation:

When I first got into investing, I asked my older brother for some advice. He said, "For starters, realize that I've been investing for 15 years and I know virtually nothing. You, of course, know less than me. And we both know more than the brokers!"

He continued, "If brokers or the guys who work at asset management companies actually knew what they were doing, or if what they were telling you was profitable a high percentage of the time, they would all invest in their own recommendations and be richer than anyone we know by now. But they're not. They're still selling you whatever their bosses tell them to sell you. That tells me their advice is wrong far too often and it's not worth listening to."

BROKERAGE FIRMS, MONEY MANAGEMENT FIRMS, AND FINANCIAL PLANNING FIRMS

All of these supposedly venerable institutions work hard on their marketing plans. They may trot out their biggest winners over the past year or two until you wonder why you were not invested in those things years ago. Or they may sell you a simple plan (oh, but that there could be a simple plan) to effortlessly get rich over time. They give you a glowy picture of what your retirement years could look like, in percentages and dollar bills, and lay before you a yellow brick road built on charts and graphs. Surely you, too, will find financial peace and freedom (just like they have?) if you give them all your money and follow these easy steps. Step 1: Don't blame them if you lose a lot of money.

After all, didn't your friend's great grandfather invest in some stocks in the 1940s, buy and hold them through bear markets, and become a multimillionaire? This surely can happen to you as well (assuming past performance is a reliable guarantee of future results, which of course never happens).

They tell you they will care about your individual concerns and needs and will cater to your desires. (This may be true as long as you don't try to take your money back.)

You may indeed find a fit for your personal style. You may find a broker who has been the family broker for 35 years, or an ally, a kindred spirit who really does care about you and your family. You may find an honest firm that does as well as can be expected when the markets blow up in everyone's face, as they do from time to time.

But this should be the bottom line question to any financial adviser: When the markets lose 30 to 40 percent, as they historically do from time to time, how are you going to hedge my risk?

"Bonds," they will say. But bonds hedge risk only in certain economic scenarios, unless you hold them to term and happen to outperform inflation.

You also should ask them what would have happened to their proposed portfolio in the mid-1970s, when selling bonds you owned before maturity would often have lost you a great deal of money, but holding them to term would not have kept up with inflation? Six-to-12-month CDs were outperforming bonds, equities, and most real estate, too.

Or in the 1930s, many of the businesses backing the corporate bonds sector that your broker will offer were going bankrupt. What if that were to happen again? Don't they believe in buy and hold?

What may have worked in the 2000–2002 bear market will likely not work in the next bear market. But again, they will likely show you only the performance graphs of the few things that did survive the last time. How many investors were actually in that exact portfolio of assets they are laying out before you, is a question they may not want you to ask.

No one knows what will do well in the next bear market. Gold, oil, bonds, Asia, nanotech, biotech, one or all may, or may not, find success in the coming decade. Their success over a longer period of time may seem like a logical prediction. But all of them will very likely lose 30 to 50 percent at some point along the way.

Tell your adviser to show you all of the programs they were selling in 1999, just before the bear market began. How much did some of those accounts lose from peak to trough through 2002? Why didn't they sell their clients the same conservative programs they are offering you now, back in 2000? Don't they believe in buy and hold?

Bottom line: Would you be comfortable with losses of 30 percent or more to your account?

If so, you are a candidate for brokerage accounts and baskets of mutual funds.

If not, you're not likely a candidate.

Financial Planners

There are many good financial planners, but the problem is they all want to get paid. And the "making money thing" can often go contrary to their best intentions. Imagine if all the pharmaceutical companies paid commissions to doctors through vacations, gifts, and the like to incentivize them to sell their drugs to one and all. No need to imagine, really. It happens.

Similarly, financial planners may get paid by insurance companies to sell life insurance and a variety of annuity products, which often are terrible plans with huge surrender fees. They are also often paid percentages of up-front fees by mutual funds that *you* end up paying, called loads, whereas similar mutual funds with no loads have the same or better performance without up-front load fees.

Some financial planners will work up a book-thick 10-year financial and retirement plan for you for a mere $5,000. But three to five years from now your life won't look anything like what you are currently projecting it to be, because, well, life is rarely that predictable.

So again, despite the fact that many financial planners have valuable skills to offer, it may not be worth the results, or the costs to gather the intellectual information.

Mutual Funds and Portfolios of Stocks

No mutual funds or stocks are predictable when trying to assess future volatility or growth. They are not the Rolls-Royce we are looking for in the risk/reward spectrum of high-net-worth investing.

It makes sense to remember two points:

1. Looking at past performance to assess future performance is statistically an almost guaranteed losing strategy.
2. Diversifying with typical financial advisers' models based on modern portfolio theory only diversifies your growth. It does not protect you against potential severe losses during bear markets (which are historically frequent occurrences). In most world crises, and in almost all secular bear markets, ships either sink all at once, or one at a time over the course of years until all ships have sunk. Clients have said to me, "My adviser diversified me with bonds and stocks and mutual funds and I lost only 20 percent during the bear market."

    How odd someone would be complimented for losing you one-fifth of your net worth. In my world, losing 20 percent of all my money would be a nightmare. It doesn't cut it.

So we must find another way, another source of profiting over the long term with lowered risk to our overall assets than unhedged investment vehicles.

Let's continue to look a bit further at the cautionary side of the equation by assessing some of the choices you will find using online financial sites, reading money magazines, watching financial TV shows, and the like:

Sector Funds

Sectors like energy, biotech, technology, real estate investment trusts (REITs), and precious metals all have had their day in the sun during the past number of years. Many newsletters will focus on one or two of these sectors and boldly declare this sector of the economy *the next great wave of profits.*

But I do not have enough faith in their or my predictions to risk putting a concentrated amount of unhedged money there. The volatility and potential risk are not worth the reward.

Exposure to these sectors is certainly warranted over the coming years and decades. But the exposure does not have to be concentrated, and should not put our assets at risk. These kinds of sector bets are in constant play in the media. Instead we can be exposed to these very same sectors in the proposed portfolios we're about to discuss, but without taking a major bet with our life savings.

International Funds

I would assume that China and India, along with other parts of Asia, will be the new growth engines of the world economy over the next 30 to 40 years. But I ask you to consider that the United States was the leader for the past 30 to 40 years, and in that time, amazing amounts of volatility, fear, downright panic, and investor pain took place during certain periods. (The 1970s, 1987, the late 1980s and early 1990s, August and September of 1998, and the early 2000s come to mind.)

Therefore, investing in China, India, and other Asian countries is not a risk-free way, a short-term way, or a surefire way to get rich, or even make any money at all. You would have to continue to buy the markets in those countries whether the markets there rise or fall over a given multiyear period, and through recessions, and realize that government instability may occur for long periods of time.

The wild card in the deck is the chance that a rebel faction might take over the government and decree that all business is now government owned! That could spell the end of your investment. And the end could happen very suddenly. (Of course, these are all worst-case scenarios. Nonetheless, it is always an investor's responsibility to consider extremes, since pendulums do swing through full cycles.)

Perhaps you could find a few broadly invested Asian-focused mutual funds that include China and India and invest in a few other broad international funds as well to spread your risk out among the rest of the world. But be prepared for many, many sharp losses along the way.

Despite the fact that India and China may be the newly declared leaders of the second half of the twenty-first century, we're not all the way there yet. And by the way, don't count the United States out just yet. It has never worked in anyone's interest to do so in the past. I do not see this country sliding into its death spiral just yet. Great countries rejuvenate and remake themselves many times over before the end of their reign, and they don't give up their economic leadership without a long, hard fight.

Hedged Mutual Funds

These are erratic, relatively new, and unproven over time. But there are a few very unique and relatively successful funds out there, some volatile, some not. You may want to try to find the best of these hedged mutual funds and diversify some of your assets among what you consider to be the best two or three of them. But their lack of correlation with the markets, their usually low performance numbers, their limited history, and/or in some cases their high volatility may eventually push you away.

U.S. Indexes

Looking in the rearview mirror, investing in U.S. indexes has worked fantastically well since the mid-1970s, with only a few bumps until the whiplash-inducing fender bender from 2000 to 2002.

The 2000 to 2002 bear market pointed out the dangers of index investing. The S&P 500 index by the end of 2006 was still down from its peak despite four years of recovery. The NASDAQ was still down over 50 percent from its peak after the same four years of recovery!

I am not convinced investing in the U.S. indexes will make investors happy or rich over the next five years.

Nonetheless, dollar cost averaging into the major indexes (see next section) may indeed still be a profitable way to invest current assets. (Note: Dollar cost averaging into a specific stock or corporate bond, or into a third world country, may not work, since it is theoretically possible for the investment to lose 90 to 100 percent of its value.)

INDEX DOLLAR COST AVERAGING: ACCUMULATING WEALTH WITH TIME

The broad U.S. indexes (specifically the S&P 500 index) have beaten all but a handful of mutual funds over almost any 10-year period. I have researched as many mutual funds and private broker managers as possible that *have* beaten the S&P consistently over the years and find no compelling reason why they might continue to do so in the future.

The major indexes are far more diversified than a typical mutual fund or basket of mutual funds.

Indexes also charge far lower annual fees than a vast majority of mutual funds.

You do not need to pay a broker, adviser, or financial planner to help you invest in this strategy while they collect big fees or commissions.

With all this taken into consideration, investing in a diversified mix of indexes may or may not make you money over the long or short term. It will certainly be volatile—too volatile for high net worth investors to risk. It will be scary at times to watch your account lose large percentages of money.

However, dollar cost averaging into indexes may offer the most viable answer as an additional growth generator for those still striving to become millionaires from their own efforts.

For those with a net worth of less than $1.5 million here is my answer to your question: "How and where should I invest my savings?"

As a nonqualified investor, until you get to the promised land of $1.5 million net worth or higher, dollar cost averaging is a great way to keep your emotions in check and hedge your bets.

The way to statistically stack the deck is to dollar cost average over a 10-to-15-year period.

Dollar cost averaging is investing a set percentage of your assets in a consistent way over a long period of time.

For instance, every January 1 and/or every July 1, you could continue to invest equal dollar amounts, or an equal percentage of your salary, to each current broad investment, whether they have gone up or down since your last investment period.

You can do this with a few good broad indexes, or even a basket of exchange-traded funds (ETFs). Just make sure you are well diversified in sectors and capitalization sizes.

If the market falls, you will be investing your next sum of money at lower prices and better valuations. It is as if you were able to turn back the clock to previous months or years.

If the market gains, you made money on the money you had invested.

To protect against a strong run-up in inflation, which is bad for both stocks and bonds, you may want to consider having some TIPS in your portfolio (inflation-adjusted bonds). Just be aware that while TIPS may limit the volatility somewhat, they could also limit the overall growth of the portfolio during a 10-year period.

Let's take an example of a dollar cost averaging approach:

If an individual had $200,000 to invest, and a steady or increasing working income yielding $50,000 of investable cash per year thereafter, I would consider investing $100,000 to begin, $100,000 six months to a year later, and $50,000 each year thereafter.

With a multiyear dollar cost average investment plan, if one can remain faithful to the plan even in the worst of times, the likelihood of profiting is high.

Dollar cost averaging combined with broad diversification provides the necessary tools for the nonqualified investor.

(Continued)

Here are some possible indexes to choose from:

1. **Most of your assets should go into either or both of these two indexes (a minimum of 50 percent and a maximum of 90 percent between the two):**

   S&P 500
   Wilshire 5000

   Remember, within these two broad indexes are REITs, oil companies, gold and precious metal companies, and all the other current darlings being hyped by the financial media. You need not feel left out. You will be invested in the biggest winning, and losing, sectors every year.

2. **10 to 25 percent of your assets should be placed internationally:**

   Use a diversified international or global index, or a big international mutual fund, such as Oakmark Global I.

3. **You might consider dollar cost averaging 0 to 20 percent of your assets into a combination of these:**

   Russell 2000 (these are small caps only and will be more volatile).

   and/or

   NASDAQ Trust (QQQQ).

   The combination of the Russell and NASDAQ should not exceed 20 percent in total.

4. You might consider dollar cost averaging 0 to 25 percent of your assets into any combination of these:

A REIT fund or REIT index, especially if you do not own your house. (REITs are real estate investment trusts.)

TIPS. Adding TIPS to your dollar cost average portfolio will reduce its growth potential. However, for those investors who want to reduce their short-term volatility, consider buying TIPS for 5 to 15 percent of your portfolio.

The goal would be to add to each of these investments on a consistent basis over at least a 10-year period.

Choose the mix according to your risk tolerance, not according to what indexes you think are going to perform better. Stay inside the percentage parameters I offered.

An aggressive mix would look like this:

25% S&P 500 index
25% Wilshire 5000 index
20% International
10% Russell 2000
10% NASDAQ (QQQQ)
10% Wilshire REIT index

A conservative mix would look like this:

30% S&P 500 index
30% Wilshire 5000 index
15% International
15% TIPS
10% REITs

(Continued)

Remember, we are not going for a 60/40 stock-to-bond ratio, or any other conservative type of traditional portfolio mix. We are going for growth and using dollar cost averaging to hedge our risk over a 10-year period or longer.

As you add money each year or semiannually, *move toward rebalancing the percentages of each index or fund you initially chose.*

I am also assuming you are not investing more than a few hundred thousand dollars in this strategy, even over time, since you would at some point likely qualify as a high net worth investor and would want to consider shifting a majority of your assets into Portfolio 2.

PORTFOLIO 2: FOR MILLIONAIRES WHO DO NOT WISH TO BECOME EX-MILLIONAIRES

Market Noncorrelation

The Great Way is not difficult for those who have no preferences.

—Third Zen Patriarch

The three keys to successful investing for investors qualified to play in the realms of hedge funds and limited partnerships are:

1. Market noncorrelation.
2. Massive diversification.
3. Intense professional due diligence.

Market noncorrelation means none of the strategies have a correlation to market direction. So part of the diversification process may mean to have some exposure, or correlation, to the markets!

Noncorrelation can markedly decrease volatility and risk under a formula that is very carefully and strictly adhered to.

Noncorrelation to the markets also means that these invest-ments are often defined as "absolute returns." This often-misused phrase means, to me, that there is a parameter of growth that can be expected regardless of the market or the economy, say within a vari-ation of +/− 3 percent. So a 10 percent expected annual return might have a variation that falls within the bracket of +7 percent to +13 percent, depending on the conditions the strategy is laboring under in a given year.

High interest rates may put some of these strategies under stress; low interest rates might put others under stress. Market volatility may be helpful to some strategies and difficult for others. But the direction of the market will not be a key indicator or driver of growth.

As I've mentioned, to noncorrelate, or hedge, from these strategies you may actually want a small percentage of market di-rectional exposure.

Some of the hedged, noncorrelated strategies I am referring to are:

- ☞ **Asset-based lending.**
- ☞ **Asset-backed securities.**
- ☞ **Collateralized debt obligations (CDOs), collateralized mort-gage obligations (CMOs), and various other debt tranches.**
- ☞ **Various other kinds of structured financing.**
- ☞ **Various forms of option trades.**
- ☞ **Hedged or timed fixed income trading.**
- ☞ **Real estate–related loans and special situations.**

☞ **Global macro trading.**
☞ **Private investments in public equity (PIPEs) funds of funds.
I would strongly advise against going into a single PIPEs
deal, or a single PIPEs fund.**
☞ **Market neutral trading.**
☞ **Long/short equity trading. This type of strategy is often dis-
appointing in bear markets but can add an important
growth component to a portfolio of diversified strategies.**
☞ **Commodities trading (though consistent success in this cat-
egory is hard to come by).**

This is by no means a comprehensive list. But these strategies are what I would typically assume to be market and index
noncorrelated. They are also to some degree noncorrelated to
each other.

These strategies can and do have periods of underperformance. These strategies all need great managers to run the
programs. Any one of these strategies will lose you money if
the manager is not extremely qualified and in fact special among
his peers.

But a group of great managers in each of these strategies may
indeed produce steady overall performances that no other investment I know of can consistently produce.

Also please note, I do not want to further define any of the
strategies in the course of this book, working under the assumption
that a little knowledge is dangerous. Suffice to say that the methodologies are complex enough to not try at home, and not trust to an
average manager. Due diligence will be the decisive factor in your
investment success with any alternative investment.

Not only are all of these strategies complex, but in reality, each
trade or loan within each fund employing these strategies would
have to be assessed in great detail before truly understanding your
risks or lack of risk. That is why only the most brilliant managers
and/or management teams can truly find an edge and produce the
kinds of absolute returns (8 to 15 percent a year with minimal

volatility and little if any market correlation) that high net worth investors should seek.

Hedge Fund Investing: Don't Try This at Home

I have mentioned the dark side of hedge funds and hedge fund investing earlier in the book (please review this section of Chapter 4 now)!

But let me also say this:

Great performance and substantial protection of principal in both good and bad markets can often coexist.

There are money managers in the world who have established trading systems and/or hedging techniques that "beat the market," or outperform their benchmark, on a consistent basis. They aren't simply working with a hot hand. They have found a systematic edge in their area of expertise.

Most of these managers require a minimum beginning investment of a million dollars. Many of them are quickly closed to new investors.

Of course, there is no guarantee of perfection with any manager, no matter how carefully chosen; nor can any manager outperform every month, every year, or in every market downturn or economic crisis.

And the fees for these investments are often indigestible at first inspection: A 1 to 2 percent management fee and a 20 percent annual fee on new profits (an "incentive fee" with a "high-water mark") are typical.

But after my best analysis:

My belief is that if an individual can diversify his or her portfolio of assets among noncorrelated groups of these world-class managers, chosen after professional due diligence, there is a strong chance of greatly reducing market risk, while optimizing the potential to powerfully grow assets over time, regardless of bear market cycles.

The many risks inherent in this type of investing have to be faced head on and dealt with right from the beginning. The best hedge funds become the best possible investments only when an investor is diversified among many different managers and the due diligence is performed by an experienced team of experts in the field.

That's where funds of funds come into play.

Funds of Hedge Funds

On February 13, 2006, the Opalesque alternative investment reporting agency released the following:

> From Investors.com: . . . About 45% of wealthy families invest in funds of hedge funds, and 84% expect to do so the next three years, says a report from Prince & Associates. . . .
>
> Pension funds tend to invest in funds of hedge funds to spread the risk. (Ken Hoover, *Investor's Business Daily*, posted 1/25/2006.)
>
> The California Public Employees' Retirement System (CalPERS), one of the nation's biggest investors, recently voted to double its hedge fund allocation to $2 billion.

Funds of hedge funds have been around for more than a decade with mixed results. In 2004 and 2005, years when hedge funds in general were not performing at optimal levels, funds of funds took a lot of the blame in the alternative financial press.

One problem constantly noted was, and is, the extra layer of fees charged by funds of funds.

What kinds of added value, if any, might the added layer of fees of funds of funds entail? If the fund of funds is doing its job, the value added can be enormous:

1. Institutional (verifiable, multisourced, professionally executed, on-site) ongoing due diligence performed on every underlying manager.
2. A far-reaching fund research network that includes third party marketers, pay sites on the Internet, and, most importantly,

word-of-mouth references or warnings about a fund from other managers, banks, and other institutional allies. Most funds of funds also do extensive personal background checks on the manager, the principals, and perhaps even the fund's accounting firm.

3. The ability to sometimes get into funds that are closed to new investors because of the fund of funds' reputation, institutional referrals, or personal relationships developed within the organization.

4. Potentially discounted fees or liquidity provisions (known as side letters) with the underlying managers. This is still possible even though new SEC regulations require more transparency regarding these kinds of side letters.

5. Assessing the legalities and language of the underlying fund documents, and analyzing audits from the underlying funds.

6. Assessing liquidity risk and other under-the-surface types of risks of the underlying fund, or of the strategy itself.

7. An experienced, steady hand moving in and out of underlying investments with a clear methodology about why the switch should occur, and where the incoming money would next be placed.

8. Some funds of funds have the ability to leverage their assets with experienced lending institutions. Of course, potential losses are magnified as well as gains. But successfully leveraging a conservative basket of hedge funds has the potential not only to mitigate the added layer of fund of funds fees and the cost of borrowing, but also to generate substantial added performance with far less risk than you would find in aggressive investments.

9. The fund of funds investor is invested in a pool of underlying managers, each of which may have million-dollar minimums. So for purposes of diversification this is also an added value. A typical fund of funds investor with $500,000 invested may be invested with 20 to 50 managers, with each manager requiring a million-dollar minimum. Since the fund of funds is the investor, the minimums were satisfied by the fund of funds long ago.

Extremely high net worth investors may be able to afford to invest in multiple million-dollar-minimum funds on their own, but even they would be hard-pressed to match the value funds of funds often provide in items 1 to 8.

The added fees funds of funds cast off, while having to be taken into consideration, should not be in and of themselves a reason to avoid investing in funds of funds.

Look past the fees to the *net returns* and decide for yourself.

The major problem with funds of funds, as I see it, really comes down to the same problem that comes with any diversified portfolio: There is either too much volatility due to too many correlated risks within the basket of underlying managers; or too little net annual return due to overdiversification (thereby reverting to the mean).

The latter is a common mistake funds of funds make when constructing their portfolios. If a fund of funds has 50 to 100 underlying managers in various strategies, then the great choices and good choices are too often muted or negated by the average and lower than average performers.

However, there are exceptions to this rule, as touched on in item number 8. Leverage applied to an average portfolio of 50 to 100 managers can create better than average performance with less risk than the market itself. Of course, manager selection becomes even more key. Losses will be magnified. But the leveraging banks are frequently overseeing the fund choices and creating careful parameters for the types of funds and styles selected and the amount of leverage they will allow: The lending bank normally has many investment parameters (haircuts) a leveraged fund of funds must stay within when assessing factors such as overall liquidity of the underlying managers, the volatility of both the individual managers and the portfolio as a whole, and a disallowing of sector or strategy concentration.

Momentum strategies based more on quantitative analysis (statistics and instinct) relative to qualitative analysis (looking into the analytics of each fund and its business model) can also show good results in the hands of a crafty fund of funds general partner who has created enough liquidity to allow him or her to switch from underperforming to outperforming managers in a timely fashion.

> Bottom line: Finding *a group* of hedged funds of funds with consistent levels of good performance net of their fees, and net of your taxes, including tolerable performances under strained market conditions, is in my opinion as close to the Holy Grail of *growth-oriented, risk-averse, passive investing* as a high net worth investor can hope for.
>
> I would say it would be most prudent to invest in a minimum of three funds of funds that correlate as little as possible with one another.

If you have over $10 million to invest, caution would say that five or more funds of funds could be in your personal portfolio, but only if they are chosen carefully. You do not want your returns to revert to the mean simply because you are overly determined to diversify.

If you have a more aggressive need for growth and some ability to dollar cost average, then a diversified basket of funds of funds (each with a different methodology but all with satisfactory past and present performance), in combination with a diversified long-only portfolio such as the ones mentioned in Portfolio 1, could be the optimum portfolio model for long-term high net worth investors. Just be careful not to be sucked into the emotional game of playing stocks or mutual funds. Use indexes and don't shoot for the moon.

A *consistent level of growth* within your entire portfolio is far more preferable than having a hodgepodge of conservative and aggressive investments that too often work against each other.

Let's compare everything I have just discussed with an unhedged strategy:

Go to a list of top-performing mutual funds for the real test.

Try a web site like Yahoo! Finance. Look up the top-performing funds since 2000. Look only at funds whose track records go back at least to 2000, and preferably back to 1998. Look at the annual performances through the bear market periods of July, August, and September of 1998 (the third quarter) and 2000–2002. Ask yourself if the good or even great returns from 2003 to 2006 or beyond were worth the risk and intense volatility in the bear market periods.

Ask yourself: Would that have been worth the risk? Look carefully at the quarterly performances. Would I have been able to remain invested? Would the emotional stress have been worth holding the funds through the bear market years? And when exactly would I have broken even from these losses?

For instance, let's take a hypothetical but not untypical top-performing fund over an eight-year period that looks like this:

1998: +10 . . . This includes a −16 percent loss in the third quarter.

1999: +34 . . . Congratulations. You are now up a compounded 47 percent in just two years.

2000: −14

2001: −12

2002: −22 . . . Your 47 percent gain just turned into a loss over five years of −13 percent.

2003: +23

2004: +12

2005: +12 . . . Your total gain over the eight-year period is 34.25 percent, or about 3.75 percent a year.

This fund would have beaten the S&P over the eight-year period by about 7 percent (34 percent versus the S&P return of about 27 percent). That would mean the S&P had an average return of less than 3.5 percent a year over the eight-year period.

If you had had the bad fortune of investing on January 1, 2000, you would have lost 40 percent of your money in three years, and still be down 24 percent in your account at the end of 2005.

With a 24 percent loss in an account, an investor needs to make about 32 percent to get back to breakeven due to the compounding of losses discussed in "The Secret Poison: Losses Overwhelm Gains" in Chapter 4.

In my evaluation, this kind of performance is simply not worth the risk, especially for high net worth investors whose goal should be to preserve principal above all else.

The goal for your portfolio is to make money, or at the very least break even, in bear market years. Additionally, we would want to see your portfolio grow nicely (10 to 15 percent annually) in a bull market. If that goal is met, your portfolio will outperform any other formula or strategy I have researched in my investment career, with far less risk and volatility.

Funds of Funds versus Multi-Strategy Funds

Some in the financial media are suggesting that multi-strategy funds are superior to funds of funds because they omit the extra layer of fees. That sounds good in principle; however, these funds will have a far smaller pool of traders to choose from. Few great traders are willing to join a firm as an employee, whereas funds of funds choose from among thousands of the best managers and traders they can find—choosing funds with existing track records, specialized expertise, and proven results.

What Should I Look For in a Fund of Funds? Low Fees, Net Performance, Good Liquidity, or All of the Above?

All of the above, without allowing higher fees or strict liquidity to rule out an investment, would be my answer.

Add this: You must really attempt to decipher why any past performance has a chance of repeating itself in the future. In other words, *What is the growth generator in the portfolio?* Let's explore.

The Biggest Risks to a Diversified Hedge Fund Portfolio

Lack of Regulations

More regulations have been enacted by the Securities and Exchange Commission (SEC) as of early 2006. But I do not see these particular regulations being very effective in preventing future fraud or theft for the most part.

For the record, I am for more regulations, not less. But they have to be effective regulations, such as those that would force certain amounts of trading transparency; disclose tax efficiency based on past years; allow limited partners far more access to the funds' accountants and auditors without having to get authorization from the general partner to request detailed information; set up clearer rules for accountability regarding a manager staying within the trading guidelines set forth in the offering documents; set liquidity guidelines that match the types of investments in the fund; create a codified due diligence process available for all limited partners and potential partners to see beyond what's in an SEC form

ADV, including easily verifiable independent background checks of the principals.

Even these few new rules would be a good start, especially if they were enacted in conjunction with voiding many of the recent regulations that are simply adding another layer of bureaucracy without getting to the heart of the potential dangers investors face.

The two biggest dangers to investors are fraud and a manager drifting away from the trading style he is portraying to investors.

When considering all of these issues, remember, there is fraud in every segment of the financial world, from financial planners to investment advisers and managers, to mutual fund managers, to individual brokers and their firms.

For hedge funds and limited partnerships, most of the regulations currently come from the individual state in which a fund is doing business, the National Association of Securities Dealers (NASD), and the SEC. These agencies could do a far better job understanding these classes of investments and the risks inherent within them. But no statistical evidence suggests that fraud is considerably more prevalent in the hedge fund industry than any other financial industry.

Lack of Due Diligence

Third party marketers of hedge funds, and hedge fund Internet sites, as a rule do *not* perform professional due diligence on the funds they promote.

Nor is professional due diligence flawless or foolproof at the end of the day.

The Dangers of Picking Funds on Your Own The problem with investors naive enough to pick high-performing or supposedly flawless hedge funds is that these reported performances may or may not be true!

Outside (independent and wholly unaffiliated) administrators are critically important to the process of confirming monthly performances.

Well-known name-brand independent auditors such as Ernst & Young and Rothstein Kass are critically important for confirming annual performances.

But occasionally even they can be fooled.

And if the investor is choosing only "great" funds—those with high performance numbers and consistent returns—as the criteria, guess what?

You have chosen one of five types of managers:

1. All the best managers.
2. All the managers with the hottest hands who will not be able to repeat their luck.
3. Managers who have good performance numbers but whose net after-tax returns to you are significantly worse than you may realize.
4. Managers who will soon revert to the mean because their funds' assets are growing too large or too fast for their trading systems or their businesses to handle.
5. All the fraudulent funds, managed by sociopaths, crooks, the desperate who cannot come to terms with their failure, and scam artists.

Add to this mix that the great managers (#1) often have very high minimums and/or are closed to new investors, and the choices shrink even further.

This is why I strongly urge you to not try this at home! Do not rely on anyone but highly experienced professionals with access to powerful due diligence teams to help decipher the #1's from the #2's through #5's.

Poor Liquidity

Another drawback to hedge fund investing (and virtually all limited partnerships) is liquidity, or to put it simply—when and how to get your money back!

There are often good reasons why hedge funds would have restricted liquidity, such as "95 days notice on the quarter with a one-year lockup."

The funds themselves may often make illiquid investments. It could be that they lend the money with a one-to-two-year repayment schedule. It could be they've invested in illiquid securities—stock positions long or short that will take more than 30 days to sell out of without incurring a major loss to the stock price on the way out. Typically these would be in the small-cap, micro-cap, and nano-cap space. Sometimes they may even include penny stocks or venture capital risk.

Other times, fund managers just want to hold on to the money for as long as possible to ensure they collect their management fees for the longest period of time they can!

Although liquidity is always a consideration, it should not normally be a determining factor in your investment process. You would be ignoring too many of the types of funds that do not correlate to the market or to each other—investments that lend money, invest in real estate, and so forth. Assume this to be a *maximum* acceptable liquidity period:

A requirement of 95 days notice on the quarter with a one-year lockup, and a 15 percent "gate" in a liquidity emergency. Capital normally returned within 30 days of the withdrawal date.

All hedge funds have a provision whereby if the markets themselves become illiquid or the fund has become illiquid the general partner can freeze the fund assets. But that would be an extraordinary circumstance, at which time attorneys would become involved. Nonetheless, for the general partner's protection this is standard language.

Limited Partnership Taxes

Assess each of your funds of funds' net after-tax performances, found on their previous years' K-1s. You should do this with the help of your accountant. Some funds tend to be more tax efficient than others. Some funds have tax equivalents that surpass ordinary income or short-term capital gains rates. Some funds have a tremendous amount of their deductions written in Schedule A, which is not deductible for a high-income investor and can seriously degrade the after-tax gains.

Of course, the same tax disadvantages can hold true for mutual funds or separately managed accounts. Check the tax implications of your investment *before* you invest.

What Are the Growth Generators in the Portfolio?

If an investment can't make you money, but only protect your assets, I don't consider that as having much value.

What Generates Profits?

When analyzing the performance of a fund of hedge funds, or any investment, the most crucial question to explore and understand is: What exactly has been generating the profits? If it turns out to be one hot fund inside a fund of funds, or one concentrated sector bet like energy or real estate that could stumble in the future, this has to be taken into consideration and seen equally as a risk factor versus a growth generator.

Extremely thorough professional due diligence and your

analysis of how your investment can achieve consistent growth going forward are your two biggest responsibilities as an investor.

Again, that is why finding a group of consistent, risk-averse funds of funds with experienced, successful general partners may be the best portfolio for high net worth investors.

You will likely be well diversified among dozens of hedge funds that have been analyzed with professional due diligence, with the general partners of each of those funds of funds incentivized to keep the performance and quality of the managers at peak levels so they can continue collecting their performance fees.

Then your responsibility need only be to focus on your research and due diligence of the funds of funds firms, their tax consequences, and their performances.

This is a far simpler and far safer route than choosing individual hedge funds on your own.

Charts, Graphs, and Back-Tests

As for charts of the efficient frontier and graphs filled with Sharpe ratios that go back just a few years, I would think their only real value would be to start good fires in the wintertime. (Note: Do not ball them up too tightly.)

As previously stated, I would include most newsletters and all trading systems for sale in this category as well.

I have also seen many back-tested strategies (where the performance is gathered by working the strategy backwards through time). I have not yet seen a back-test that worked into the future as well as it worked in the past. They may serve as a frame of reference to some very sophisticated investors. But that would be their maximum benefit.

See the Appendix for a sample fund of funds questionnaire—
one that an institutional investor might submit to a prospective
fund of funds before investing.

Combining a Hedged Portfolio with a Dollar Cost Average Market Correlation Strategy

There are times when aligning 5 to 20 percent of your portfolio
with the direction of the stock market may be a wise consideration
as a multiyear investment. After all, the dark side of the stock market, discussed in Chapter 4, has to be weighed against what happens
in great (secular or long-term) bull markets.

Timing the market is the key, but as I've said, in my research I
have found short-term timing systems to be elusive and longer-
term systems to be imperfect.

When the timing game is the only one you're playing, there is
no hedge against a mistaken call. That is not acceptable in my investing paradigm.

Macro-Timing of Secular Bull Markets

The one model that I think is appropriate to consider is the macro-
timing of U.S. markets based on the valuation of forward earnings
of the S&P 500.

Secular bull markets begin when those price-earnings (P/E)
levels approach 12. They have gone as low as 7 (in the mid-1970s).
The average P/E is 16. At the beginning of 2007 the P/E was around
18 to 19. No long-term (secular) bull market has ever been
launched from a P/E that high. Therefore, having zero percent of
your portfolio in market-correlated investments during an overvalued period such as that makes sense.

However, someday the P/E level on the S&P will again approach a lower level like 12 or 14. When it does, and if virtually
everyone is calling you the world's greatest fool for considering in-

vesting even a dime of your money in the stock market, at that point you may want to consider investing 5 to 20 percent of your assets in more aggressive market-correlated hedged funds of funds, or if you are emotionally able to handle the volatility you may consider dollar cost averaging some of that 5 to 20 percent directly into the stock market. If you *do* take this risk, it must be a long-term play.

I would consider dollar cost averaging that money into indexes to be the best strategy to use during a time of reasonable to good valuation levels. (See Portfolio 1.)

You also should establish a clear selling point. I might suggest it would be at a time when the P/E on the S&P 500 rises back to 18, or perhaps even 19 (well above the P/E 16 average).

There's no telling how much further the index could rise beyond that, but you would not be staying in cash, feeling ill about pulling your money out of a rising market. You would simply shift the assets back over to noncorrelated investments. That way you always have your hedge and the potential to continue to make steady profits while you await the next clear opportunity.

As clever as this strategy may seem, I would not recommend this strategy for high net worth investors who are steadily approaching, or who have entered, the End Game. The reasons why are spelled out in the following story.

Letter to a High Net Worth Investor

Ray (fictitious name of course), a client of mine, was a fantastically brilliant real estate developer who was able to retire at age 40 with a very high net worth. He was traveling the world, learning piano, and becoming well-versed in many subjects. He was also fascinated by America and how it was seen through the eyes of the rest of the world.

It was the spring of 2006 and the war in Iraq was getting uglier by the day. Through his various conversations on his international travels he became convinced that the U.S. dollar was going to crash.

He set about finding ways to protect his vast net worth, such as buying different currencies, investing in the Australian stock market, buying gold, and investing in Japan. Most of these investments were already doing well before he invested.

Something, however, was going wrong with this strategy even while he was making money. Although he had an amassed a fortune he was consumed every day mostly with these few international investments, which in total did not equal even 20 percent of his net worth.

He was watching a financial TV show one day when he was impressed by an specialist in the field of global investing. He decided to give this manager a few million dollars. He let me know about this and asked my opinion. We spoke for a while about how it was impossible for even this manager to know if he could with certainty make Ray money. I expressed a bit more of my investment philosophy to him and he appreciated my input. Then he sent me an e-mail that said:

> FYI: I'm not going to invest any money with the foreign stock guy I saw on TV because when he finally made his recommendations to me I had a sense he didn't know what he was talking about! I think I'm more comfortable just being in cash.

This was my letter back to him:

> It's so interesting to watch you go through your decision-making process. You must realize these guys and gals are on TV, all dressed up and made up, marketing themselves to the media with the clear intention of either raising capital or trying to create a broader media image for themselves, instead of being in their offices serving their clients by overseeing their investments.
>
> In general, it's important to see through the media information and peer into what the motives behind the messages are. For instance, it's quite natural for a manager with a huge gold position (a

very, very risky thing to do, and a big, volatile bet to make) to go on a financial TV show, if he can get on, and make his best case for gold going to 5,000. He would love nothing better than to create a mania: "So and so is claiming gold is going to 5,000—how outrageous." Meanwhile you're thinking, "Well, it's at 650 now; if I buy it and it only goes to 3,000, that's okay!" The problem is, more often than not gold goes up only another 2 percent and then has seen its high for the year!

I like your comment of being comfortable with cash. We *are* in an inflationary period, but also a period where real estate and housing may be right on the cusp of unwinding from their sky-high valuations. It's likely to be a good time to continue to invest in things like conservative hedged funds of funds, if you're comfortable continuing to do so, and if you trust the firm. But it's also a good time to be comfortable with a decent amount of laddered short-term bonds and cash, and wait a few years until value appears in an asset class you are comfortable with such as real estate, or even the stock market to some degree sometime in the future.

Meanwhile, hedged funds of funds, bonds, and cash allow you to sleep at night and get on with your life, instead of watching, and fretting over, your "gold position" or "short U.S. dollar" position over coffee every morning.

Because remember: Neither a great win nor a great loss in any or all of your gold or dollar or Asia positions will change your life for the better or for the worse. They could triple or go to zero. Your financial life will remain mostly unchanged from what it is now.

Yet what it will do to your emotions each day—especially on days like the past few, when gold has declined strongly and the U.S. dollar has risen strongly—will not be worth *either* the win or the loss. Why put yourself through the emotional seesaws you will experience such as "I should have sold this at X or bought more of that at Y" or "Stop loss this one at Z," when you don't need to do *any of that* to live a fiscally secure life and buy whatever it is you desire? Is *that* life? Or is that a diversion not much more healthy than outright gambling—a diversion that is taking you away from a deeper and better life?

I would assume one of the reasons you worked so hard to be financially successful is that you imagined not having to *be burdened* by the things those with lesser financial means must deal with. You need not take on that burden. Not ever again! But, here you are, with a naturally creative and busy mind, suddenly finding yourself playing stockbroker/wheeler-dealer in your head each day! What exactly is the point? Even if the dollar falls dramatically and you have all U.S. dollars, exactly how affected would you be by that? I submit: *not much!*

The true bottom line is this: Who or what are you actually serving in the end by mucking around with timing asset classes and currencies??? I have seen very few human beings able to find success at that over the long run. (Many of them do win a few battles, but then lose the war.)

Time is so precious. It's not just about free time. It's about how you feel internally in that free time. If you are trying to learn piano and all the time your mind is thinking, "Maybe I should sell Japan," *that will not serve your life in the end.*

This is my key message: One has to ask oneself,

"Am I playing the markets, or am I being played?"

"Is investing deeply enriching me and/or serving my life each day? Or is my life being kidnapped by a toxic diversion?"

My suggestion to you is to make your investing life simple: conservative hedged funds of funds, cash, and other very nonvolatile ideas like tax-free municipal bonds run by a qualified bond broker Then you walk away a free man! Plus you walk away with investments that make sense for a high net worth individual.

But if you continue to play this game day to day, even on the fringes, the game too often ends up playing you. That's what happens over and over again—even to the best of us.

8

Hedge Fund Mind-Set

ADDRESSING INVESTORS' QUESTIONS FROM PART TWO

There seems to be a common perception that hedge funds trade mostly stocks and are extremely risky, which brings up a more direct question: Exactly how do you define "hedge funds"?

My unofficial definition of a hedge fund is that it's just another name for a limited partnership (LP) or a limited liability company (LLC) that can pretty much do whatever it wants to do within the confines of the law. It can invest in loans, real estate, oil and gas, commodities, options, and/or mortgages. Or a manager could go on margin and short Google and then go to the movies. Many hedge funds are very risky, while others are poor investments for different reasons. But still others are managed by brilliant conservative-minded firms that know their strategy and their space and have found an edge. The point is there is a massive array of investing concepts within the format of hedge funds.

How does an investor choose among the thousands of fund offerings? Selecting the funds with the best past returns, like in the mutual fund world, seems to be the equivalent of fool's gold.

I think funds of funds managers are crucial arbiters between the investors and the funds themselves, to assess the quality, legitimacy, and possible future performance—rather than past performance—of what is being offered.

In the past 10 years there is no doubt in my mind that hedge funds have transformed the world's markets. They have been embraced by high net worth investors, pension funds, and endowments worldwide, and are now recognized as an asset class in their own right.

I think that well-managed funds of funds are the workhorses behind the growth and legitimacy of the industry—usually upholding institutional due diligence standards and insisting on certain partner protections that individuals do not have the experience, quantity of assets, time, or manpower to establish on their own. About 40 percent of the approximate $2 trillion presently invested in hedge funds is funds of funds money.

What first led you to the idea of investing in hedge funds and funds of funds?

Reading about the history of the U.S. and world stock markets, I clearly came to see the massive dangers there—and that when they fall hard they can break family fortunes that were hard-won over a number of generations. The dangers will come and come again. I also understand there is greatness in the markets. The best opportunities in the world can arise from equity investing from time to time. And I understand there is danger in every other investment vehicle on earth, not just the stock market.

Certainly many, even most, hedge funds are nothing I would ever invest in. Yet, in the end, I came to believe that the best hedge funds in the world are the best investments in the world. On a risk/reward basis, they are hard to compete against over any multiyear period.

But the best hedge funds become the best possible investments only when an investor is diversified among many different managers and the due diligence is professionally handled by an experienced team. That's where funds of funds come in.

Just as the markets have risk, hedge funds are susceptible to sudden and unforeseen risks in their particular niche market, and there are nonmarket risks that can be mitigated only by diversification, ongoing professional due diligence, and any other way you can find to protect yourself.

I read somewhere that there are now nearly 5,000 hedge funds. How many of them are on your radar?

There are actually about 8,500 hedge funds, according to the most current statistics I have seen (11,000 if you include funds of funds). Some hedge funds are mom-and-pop operations. I won't even look twice at 99 percent of them, because I have very strict initial criteria before I even look at performance: Those criteria include the fund having a manager with a reputable background, more than just a few million dollars under management in the firm, a strong back office, and an independent auditor and administrator. After that, I look at performance, but only in context—in other words how the fund performed relative to its peers in the same or a similar strategy. Then the due diligence period becomes very intense and remains ongoing throughout the life of the investment. By the time I look at all of those factors, there are probably less than 500 funds out of the 8,500 that I even keep on my radar for future assessment.

How do you respond to some people's comments that hedge funds are not being regulated and therefore are more dangerous than mutual funds?

I wish they were more regulated, but that the regulations were more tuned in. For instance, I believe all hedge funds, and funds of funds, should be required to have independent auditors and administrators. All individual funds should be required to have transparency to some degree—say a representative 10 to 20 percent of their portfolio from the previous quarter—just to make sure they are doing what they say they are doing. All funds should be required to allow partners to speak with the administrator or accountant or auditor without prior consent from the manager. After all, they are literally partners. . . . So much more could be done.

However, the percentage of rip-offs in the hedge fund industry does not by any means go beyond the percentage of fraud and theft that happens in the traditional investment world, where regulations abound.

I think this is because many regulations are the wrong kinds of regulations. But also people, especially devious or desperate people, can go outside of any regulation until they're caught. Those who propose and vote on new regulations should know the ways in which the fox can put himself in a position to guard the chicken coop. The chickens in this metaphor are the investors.

We can't leave everything to regulations. We want to make sure we pick managers who know how to be a fox in their particular niche market, but also a protector of the limited partners' money, and open to sharing their internal fund information with their limited partners and the Securities and Exchange Commission (SEC), all at the same time. Legitimate operations have nothing to hide. But regulators need to get to the heart of the matter and not waste everyone's time and taxpayer money.

They can do this by simply creating laws that open up the books of the funds and give open access to the funds' prime brokers and accountants to the limited partners, and to their attorneys at any time.

Limited partners should have the right to talk to their funds' prime brokers or accountants or auditors and say, "I am hearing X from the manager; can you confirm that?" A simple yes or no would suffice. That alone would prevent most of what the regulators fear without the regulators themselves getting directly involved or creating another massive set of ineffective laws.

Discuss in more detail what good or great due diligence entails, and why you feel the average investor should not do this on his or her own.

Due diligence includes office visits; background checks; assessments regarding the quality and quantity of back office staff; and assessments of the quality of the fund's administrator, auditor, attorney firm, prime broker, and methodology. With many funds of funds, portfolio transparency is requested from the underlying managers and often received simply because the investor is institutional, rather than a single investor whose motives they cannot be sure of. Funds of funds may also start with a $5 million to $10 million position, instead of $250,000. So the managers tend to be more receptive to invasive kinds of requests like transparency.

For similar reasons, funds of funds can sometimes get some sort of negotiated discount on fees, liquidity, or other issues of concern.

In many cases there is power in size. Often, smaller amounts of assets greatly decrease diversification, but also decrease the ability to negotiate terms or to add protection to a portfolio like an overarching fraud and theft insurance protection policy does.

The other important reason I think an investor should not invest in single hedge funds on his or her own is because of the sheer expense of thorough professional due diligence. It is quite prohibitive and extraordinarily time-consuming on an ongoing basis.

Even with professional due diligence, I do not think individuals should ever have more than 10 percent of their total assets in a given single hedge fund, regardless of how tempting it might seem.

USING ETIQUETTE, RECEIVING RESPECT: THE GENERAL PARTNER/LIMITED PARTNER RELATIONSHIP

The communication between the general partner (the manager) of a fund of funds (or single fund) and the limited partner (investor—you) has some fairly clear parameters that I can share with you so that you can maximize your role as the manager of your own assets.

The first thing that goes without saying is that you and/or an attorney with hedge fund experience should read the fund documents. Within them are the terms of the agreement.

The terms will include the big four:

1. Withdrawal provisions.
2. Entry points.
3. Withholding period of a percentage of redeemed assets until after the audit (5 to 10 percent is normal).
4. Fee structure.

Also in the documents should be the names of the firm's attorney and accountants and/or auditors. They should be called before you invest. (See Appendix at the back of this book.)

Don't invest in any fund or manager that seems put off by your initial questions and due diligence. (Again, see Appendix for more about the due diligence process.) However, if your inquiries go on for longer than a few months, the firm will probably begin to treat you as a "crying wolf" type of investor who may ask questions incessantly and then never be heard from again. So make your inquiries concise. If you are not interested enough to invest after a month or two of investigation, stop the process and move on.

Your inquiries about which funds the firm is invested in or what percentage each fund represents in the portfolio may be met with some hesitation by the firm. The managers do not want investors or other firms stealing these names, then investing directly in these managers after all the research and due diligence they have done. The firm survives on fees paid by investors for their expertise in the research and due diligence field. But it is certainly justifiable and in fact your responsibility to know at least once or twice a year:

☞ What each of the underlying managers is invested in and what percentage of the portfolio it currently represents (e.g., Manager A is a 2 percent position and is invested in equities long/short).

☞ What the portfolio as a single entity is focused on, and what kind or risk/reward parameters the firm foresees under various market conditions.

☞ Whether the focus or risk/reward parameters changed over the past 6 to 12 months.

Of course, you as the investor have every right to know what the performance of the fund is, and how your account is doing. What's appropriate is to know by the 10th of each following month what the estimated performance *was for that month net of fees*. Many funds will also offer midmonth rough estimates. Estimates and rough estimates may be off by as much as 0.5 percent to even 1 percent, but good funds tend to underestimate ballpark returns.

What is *not* appropriate is to request estimates more accurate than within 0.5 percent (funds of funds are compiling underlying fund performances that often change by a few basis points by the time the final number is received, which in turn will skew the fund of funds number).

It is also not appropriate to expect daily or even weekly performance updates from a fund of funds, or to constantly call the manager with questions or concerns about the market, the funds, or your account. If you do not like the performance over a six-month period, consider withdrawing. But complaining, or "processing through things" with the manager will simply put your relationship with him or her under pressure.

It is certainly a normal and positive thing to assess and discuss fund performance with a manager once or twice a year. And it is always within your rights to withdraw if the expectation the manager and you originally had for the fund is not being met.

Try to establish and continue a friendly relationship with the manager of the firm. Ask about his or her perception of market conditions a few times a year and track them for accuracy over time. It is not your job, nor will it serve you in any way, to debate the manager's performance with him or her. If you come to a point where you do not see eye to eye you always have the right to withdraw.

You should receive your account information quarterly or monthly (usually with a delay of four to six weeks since it is a fund of funds). The account statement must come *directly* from the fund administrator or accountant, who in turn *must be independent* of the fund of funds firm itself; that is, they must be receiving independent performance reports from the fund's underlying managers. If the fund is generating *in-house* statements, or no statements, don't invest.

Your receipt of K-1s may be delayed well past the April 15 tax deadline, sometimes by months. This is not uncommon and you should expect to file for an extension.

Let your accountant do the work of processing the K-1s for the IRS. Do not ever try to do your own accounting at this level of complexity unless you are a professional CPA. Make sure the accountant you choose to work with has experience with hedge fund K-1s.

It is critical you create and maintain a good working relationship with the manager and other representatives at the firm. Relationships should be somewhere between cordial and downright friendly. If you feel you are not treated with 100 percent respect, discuss it once if you wish, to see if the relationship gets better, or withdraw. It's not the responsibility of the managers to become friends with you. But it is their responsibility to be amicable, polite, respectful, honest, and open about the fund's goals and future direction.

If a manager or a high-up representative outright lies to you, even once, withdraw immediately.

The Ultimate Risk/Reward Mind-Set for High Net Worth Investors

The key to a successful portfolio is to not lose money. A return of pretax 8 to 10 percent annually *with very little volatility* might be a typical goal for someone with $2 million or more invested throughout a full bull and bear market cycle.

A portfolio of well-managed funds of funds can help achieve this goal. Avoiding aggressive investments is critical so that *your entire portfolio, seen as one diversified investment*, can reach this target.

The more you lose in an aggressive investment, the more responsibility you put on your other investments to recover those losses. In the end, this is a game too emotionally frustrating, financially risky, and statistically difficult to win.

Someone told me the poet Robert Stafford was once asked by an interviewer how many poems he wrote per year.

He replied that he wrote 365 poems.

The interviewer was amazed. "My God, you write an average of one poem a day?"

Stafford said, "Yes, every morning I get up, go to my desk, and write a poem."

The interviewer then asked, "What is the secret of such prolific creativity?"

Stafford was said to have answered: "Lowered expectations."

Lowered expectations is the wise mind-set to adopt when your net worth allows you to live off of the income of a pretax 8 to 12 percent a year.

Part Four

PLANNING FOR THE FUTURE AND SEEKING THE END GAME

9

The Financial Planning Maze

Many financial planners charge $5,000 or more to develop a retirement plan, or a five-year plan, for you and your family.

You will receive a nice thick brochure with numbers in it.

Separate each page carefully.

You now have a high number of potential paper airplanes.

I was at a meditation retreat several years ago with a great Buddhist teacher named Jack Kornfield. He asked us to do a series of one-minute meditations about the following:

☞ What do you envision your life will be like in six months?
☞ What do you envision your life will be like in one year?
☞ Then five years?
☞ Then 10 years?

When we had completed the meditations, Jack said, "One thing I can guarantee each of you: Whatever you were thinking, that won't be what happens."

Life is very much like the stock market itself: It is strange and volatile. At its core is an impenetrable mystery that no one has been able to decode. It presents massive obstacles and great opportunities, none of which could have been predicted or set up by going down a prescribed course.

So the odds of a retirement plan or a five-year plan actually coming to pass is, like Jack Kornfield supposed, virtually zero. And unless you like expensive paper airplanes, you will be wasting your time and money trying to find value within your plan's hallowed pages of statistics and graphs.

HOW TO PLAN FOR THE FUTURE: A SIMPLE THREE-STEP PROGRAM

Step 1: Savings Neutral Phase

Your annual income from investments, salary, and other earnings— *not including increases in the value of your primary residence*—as a goal should at least equal your overall annual expenses.

This brings you to a place that I call the **savings neutral phase.** Stay cautious and don't assume added debt just because you have X amount of dollars in liquid assets. The reality is you're living month to month!

Step 2: Rebuilding Phase

In years when you fall short of the goal in step 1, the new goal would be to replenish the shortfall in future years by decreasing your spending and your need for material items, increasing your family earnings by working more, and so on. This is what I call the **rebuilding phase.**

Note: Do not get more aggressive with your investments to make up for problems that are essentially budgeting problems. Budgeting problems are permanent problems until you address what is at the heart of problem—overspending. Aggressive investing can only work sporadically. The minute you try to address a budgeting problem by increasing your investment risk you are back in the casino, and you are assuming you will beat the casino virtually *every year!* That is statistically and actuarially next to impossible.

Step 3: Growth Phase

In years when there is a substantial increase in your income beyond your expenses (including investment income, but not real estate equity from your primary residence):

☞ Consider some or all of the increase a part of your new principal base that you do not want to diminish in the future.
☞ Take some or part of the increase and spend it.
☞ Tag some or all of the increase for a future goal such as your children's college educations or buying a more expensive house (using the windfall for the down payment if you can then afford the mortgage payments).
☞ Combine some of the above ideas.

I call step 3 the **growth phase**. It would be nice if we were all in the growth phase every year. But we must assume life is tricky and not overestimate our future potential growth.

Remember to include the annual taxes you must pay before you spend the excess profits!

These three phases, though obvious at first blush, are really the core of all good financial planning. Clear benchmarks are set for whatever phase you and your family may be in. And since we have no idea what the next year will bring, we may well encounter each phase at least once in our lives, no matter which stage we are starting from.

FAMILY BUDGETING: SECURING PRESENT ASSETS WHILE HAVING FUN

Who gets to make up the budget in your family? Or don't you have one?

I suggest you establish a budget regardless of how wealthy or poor you might be. I would suggest the budgeting process be a joint effort if you are married.

If you have after-tax income exceeding your expenses and you are a qualified investor, under typical circumstances it's time to live it up a bit. Do indulge yourself. Enjoy life, and make sure your spouse enjoys life as well.

Do not assume taxes in your budget. If you made no income from work or your investments you would have no tax. So it will be something you will just have to net out of your gross income each year.

Do try to at least imagine what phase you may be in for the following year. If there is likely to be less income, then pull back your generosity and fun now to prepare for that. If your income will remain the same or be even better, then allow an appropriate amount of joy and excess to be a part of your budgeted living expenses.

> Bottom line: If you are a qualified investor and are not eating away at your principal year by year, then be sure to budget in *fun*. The amount of money you can take with you when you die is less than one penny. Don't be cheap with yourself or your family. Live the good life *as long as you are not touching your principal.*

SEEING LIFE, BUSINESS, AND INVESTING AS ONE PORTFOLIO

Each day or two at the very least, something must draw you out of the world of money and finance and back into a place of heart and creativity: the other dimensions and the deeper purposes in life.

People can be deadened by the "money as the cultural totem" experience, and become addicted to the time that one must spend to be successful at *both* work and investing. It can lead to a certain feeling of detachment from real life and a deadness that certainly does not match the symbol of what it's like to be rich or successful. This disconnect of image and reality can make the situation feel even worse.

This deadness of the spirit (even if success is occurring in one's business and investments) must be addressed head-on and immediately. It is a disease of terminal proportions. It is no less of a warning sign than your business itself going into the red.

Here is an interesting mathematical equation to consider:

☞ Your financial and work life—your job and/or business and your investing—should eventually take up no more than half of your overall waking time and attention.
☞ Being connected to your own spiritual and creative forces, and taking care of your health with exercise and eating right, should account for at least one-half of your waking time and attention.
☞ And your spouse and children and/or close friends should account for at least one-half of your waking time and attention.

This "Yogi Berra math" serves to give us a very good perspective on things: There never seems to be enough time for everything. And there isn't. Yet each of these things must be attended to in these approximate proportions, at the very least!

Certainly there is a time and season, an ebb and flow, when one of these matters overwhelms the others for a while. But it often comes back to balancing the art and the craft of life.

The art of life comes from exploring our creativity, searching for our own sense of spirit or faith, seeking out affiliations in our business life, and sharing the credit and the wealth that comes our way with those who helped us get there.

The craft is having your finances and your business organized enough, safe enough, and delegated enough to allow you to look ahead and plan ahead.

But the planning would involve far more than business or investing plans. The plans I'm alluding to would be about turning your life goals and dreams into reality.

Because when you stop to think about it:

Spending all your time thinking about your money *is a terrible waste of the money.*

10

The Game Beyond the End Game

Once your ability as a craftsman has allowed the art of your life to come front and center, you are at the Game Beyond the End Game!

The Game Beyond the End Game focuses on what gives you joy, not just the highest number of dollars.

It is based on wholeness, not just increasing how many generations you can support with your wealth.

Having your children seeing you live as an integrated human being is a far greater legacy to leave than money and real estate.

Once the Game Beyond the End Game is defined as such, we discover this new shift in thinking offers us a more profound and joyous life experience, win or lose.

> Here is a true Game Beyond the End Game story—one I heard in New Mexico one rainy night as told by an Indian saint named Amma:
>
> Once there was a man who was very proud of his business. He supported his family and supplied them
>
> *(Continued)*

with all the material items they needed. But in order to do this he had to work many nights as well as working all day, and three-quarters of all the holidays as well.

One Saturday morning as he was going off to work his wife reminded him that it was his son's ninth birthday. He went to his son and asked, "Would you like to go to the circus today as your birthday gift?" The son responded, "Are you coming with me?" The father said he had to work, but that he would get the boy and his mother front-row seats. His son said in that case he preferred not to go.

His father offered him many other gifts if he would only go with his mother. But the son refused them all. Finally, the father agreed to delay the work he had to do until that evening and go to the circus with his son.

At the circus he noticed his son laughing at each of the scenes. The boy was certainly enjoying himself. It was a winter day and it began to snow. Wind entered the circus tent and the father became cold. He put his winter coat on, and in a further attempt to get warm he wrapped his son in the coat with him as they watched the final act.

On the way home the businessman said, "You certainly seemed to enjoy yourself. You laughed at all the scenes. What did you enjoy the most?" The son replied without hesitation, "When you wrapped me up in your coat."

The businessman/father began to weep. He was embarrassed by this and hugged his son against his body to prevent the son from seeing him cry.

But then as he did so his life began to flash by his closed eyes. He saw so much of his time being wasted by busy-ness. So much of his time was being spent avoiding his family responsibilities, and then paying his family off with some of the money he earned.

But this intimacy he was experiencing now with his son, this feeling of family and of an overall sense of love and compassion, far surpassed anything he had ever felt in any of his business world victories.

He had been wasting so many precious moments while his son had grown from a baby to nine years old in the blink of an eye. And now, now, he realized he had to find a way to make it up to his family and pay them back somehow.

DOWNSIZING THE AMERICAN DREAM

When she was six years old, my daughter once asked an Indian swami, "Swami, is this all just God's dream?"

The swami replied, "No Annabel, this is *your* dream. And when you wake up, you'll see God."

The American dream has a similar metaphor:

You could ask, "Is the American dream of material wealth *my* dream?"

And (metaphorically I am a swami now!) I would say: "If it is, it will be a nightmare as well as a dream."

Dreams of material wealth can put you to sleep, or drive you crazy!

They can rob you of pure joy. They can entangle you in the nightmares of repairing these material dreams when they break, and they can fill your days with worries about things being ruined, stolen, losing their value. You get the picture.

But when you wake up and keep life in perspective you have the potential to find the joy the American dream promised you. Because money is an amazing gift as well.

To wake up inside, we have to recognize that this dream of wealth and material ownership is the culture's dream, but on a personal level it rarely works long-term. A person is not born to simply follow the culture's dream. Inventions and great entrepreneurial successes do not occur by simply following the culture's dream. They are created by breaking out of the dream and finding a new path.

It becomes even worse if you reach out for the culture's dream before you can afford to. You then may take on the stress and craziness of trying to make it work out by constantly getting lucky and pulling rabbits out of your hat. (And I can tell you that no one I know has ever found a real rabbit in their hat, ever. So the odds are not good you will.)

I once knew a couple so hungry for the American dream that they maxed out all their credit cards while both of them were working around the clock with their eight-month-old daughter in day care five days a week. I'm sure you know people in similar circumstances. Is this a "dream" life? Or is this a nightmare that in many ways they brought upon themselves?

I have a dream I have been following. My dream is to access as much creative energy, joy, love, and compassion as I am able to, hour by hour each day, as long as I am being responsible to my health, the ones I love, the people I work with, and my family's financial well-being. (It's a dream that is actually very close to Abraham Lincoln's speech immortalized at the Lincoln Memorial in Washington, D.C.)

Therefore, I came up with my new fiscal/life philosophy: relative downsizing.

RELATIVE DOWNSIZING

Relative downsizing does not mean kicking all of your relatives out of the house!

It involves kicking all the cultural ideas about how to live, and what you are supposed to need to have a rich life, out of your house, so you can start from scratch without interference from the TV, your neighbors, your parents, or anyone else, until what is left in your house is mostly just pure *fun*.

Relative downsizing means that at every stage of your financial life you might consider downsizing your material and financial *goals* to make life easier on yourself.

I didn't say abandon material and financial goals. Just tone them down to fit you so you are not chasing some ghost of happiness down a dark road to nowhere.

Let's look at a few theoretical stages.

Stage 1: You are working and playing by the rules, making $100,000 a year with $100,000 in savings. You are almost ready to buy your first small house. You don't need $5,000 couches, a hot new car, a built-in pool, or a wardrobe that would make a Hollywood star feel right at home. You want a moderately priced car (maybe a hybrid!) and furniture that is modest. Aim your material goals to match your lifestyle, but *not to add stress to your life*. Downsize your goals to allow your savings to continue to grow until you have enough to invest a few hundred thousand dollars safely. Then you will be at the next stage. If you do not downsize your material goals now you may not make it to the next level. Create a cautious budget. The trapdoor, the wild card that will throw you back into the financial dungeon from whence you came, is *debt*. Excluding a potential affordable car loan, and your mortgage debt, which is necessary but should be affordable on a monthly basis, make sure you have *zero* debt.

Pay off credit cards on time every month without fail. Remember: Time is the most cherished thing on earth. Free time is a sought-after commodity even by the ultrarich. Make sure you are the envy of all the overworked and overstressed millionaires on earth. You don't get to the next level of wealth by working three jobs and maxing out your credit cards. You get to the next level of wealth by becoming better and better at the job you have, earning more money, and living simply . . . for now.

Stage 2: You are making $200,000 a year with $200,000 in savings. You own a house. Are you ready for a new car? Okay. But don't buy a Porsche . . . yet. Try a BMW (or a higher-end hybrid)! Nicer furniture might be in the cards, but no boats, horses, or mansions. Those are reserved for when you are a multimillionaire, if you want the headaches that come with them. In the meantime, begin a serious investing program. And create a retirement plan that makes sense at least for now. There are always emergency plans for your old age like reverse mortgages to add into the mix. But the key goal right now would be to live beneath your means to a great degree and clear the way to become a certified millionaire.

Stage 3: You are a millionaire at last. The first million is the hardest million to make! Celebrate a bit. It may be time to upgrade your house, especially if the housing market is undervalued. Try to hold your material purchases down below the level of having to constantly take care of your toys. Keep those items to a minimum. Keep your eye on the goal of getting better at your work, finding ways to enjoy your work, and creating free time for yourself. The Game Beyond the End Game is about creating free time so that it can be filled with things you and your family choose to do, not things that people or entities outside the family are demanding from you. Be sure to have enough time for your kids. If you want to leave an inheritance for your children, wrap them in your coat now, not when they are in their 30s. The most valuable inheritance is a seed planted in a child's heart, not a check wired from your account to theirs.

Stage 4: You are a multimillionaire. It is now time to consider the power broker aspect of being rich. You are no longer forced to invest all your money in order to plan for your retirement and your family's future. Make sure free time is your most valued asset, and that material purchases do not cost you more time or cause you more upset than pleasure. It's time for the Porsche now, but do test-drive it and make sure you like it better than a hybrid! Be honest with yourself. You may decide it's not as much fun to actually drive as the dream of driving it was. Take pleasure in buying things that help you feel free, or owning a modestly priced car that creates a new trend, if you prefer that as a lifestyle choice. Stand on your own and create your own sense of taste. You are now setting the trends, not following them. Make sure you have an accountant and an estate attorney who can work together and shift gears as events and tax laws dictate. If you have a lot of capital gains on a particular asset, you might want to consider a charitable remainder trust.

Overall, you can now afford the priceless things in life. Focus on the art as well as the craft in your work. Carefully budget your time, not just your spending. Find charities that make sense to you. You cannot purchase respect or loyalty. You must be deserving from the inside out. Be a leading voice in your community for the public good. Endeavor to access your sense of compassion as well as accenting your living room with the next new high-tech television screen.

Relative downsizing means that you will always consider living somewhat below your peak means— to stay sane.

Keeping up with the Joneses may be hazardous to your life, liberty, and pursuit of happiness.

INVESTING IN THE TWENTY-FIRST CENTURY

John Mauldin first introduced me to the concept of exponential growth in the worlds of science and medicine via discussing the findings of Dr. Ray Kurzweil. These future realities will be for better and/or for worse. But having an awareness of the future is always an advantage as an investor.

The basic premise is this:

Many of the present-day baby boomers' life spans may extend into their 90s. Those now under 40 could live past 100.

And today's preteens may have an unimaginable "deathless option" if they have enough money to keep themselves aligned with the best technology of the twenty-first century.

What this does to concepts like retirement and long-term investing strategies in the next 50 years may be equally unimaginable.

The field of medical diagnostics will likely be a strong growth area for the professional money manager to choose winners from, as would be true of many other areas in the technology and biotechnology sectors.

But the losers on a pure business level will always outnumber the winners, even in the hottest sectors of the economy. Therefore, sophisticated traders and those disciplined enough to hedge their investments will still very likely have a great advantage over the buy-and-hold investors and the pure speculators.

Volatility and fiscal risk will not end, even for those on their way to becoming immortal.

Imagine having to work well into your 80s and 90s and having to plan your retirement not for a potential 20-to-30-year period, but for a 50-to-60-year period!

Or: Imagine having to work . . . forever!

What this would say to me is similar to what a present mortal life says to me:

Make sure you love your work, and make sure you do not squander your money on risky investments—because investing will be a critical link to the success of any family in this century, as it has been in centuries past.

The twenty-first century may not be about hoping for one good investment cycle to pull us through, as was so often the case in the twentieth century. The road could run far longer, and demand far deeper skill than anything we have experienced in the past.

TRANSCENDING THE CENTURIES: WHOM DO YOU SERVE?

Financial freedom is a tricky concept. How can you be free if at the same time you feel burdened to make everything work out perfectly for yourself, your family, and future generations?

Emotional freedom around money and investing is even trickier. The burdens of making, saving, investing, and spending money, and the images about being rich, are so sanctified and so intense that statistically this burden often leads to 24/7 workdays, a shorter life span, and less of a chance of achieving optimal health and energy while alive.

This seems to be an odd pay-off for such a unique and often difficult achievement as becoming rich.

Even more difficult can be understanding *why* the emotions around money affect us so strongly. Some say money is all about survival and security, while others say it's ultimately about personal power, or pure ego.

At some point during a lifetime of work and effort, deeper life questions may arise that are just too powerful to ignore: What is the point to all this? To whom are you ultimately dedicating all this effort, time, worry, money, and responsibility? Whom do you serve?

Or, to broaden the question even further, once we have accumulated enough money and material goods for our survival, our security, endless ways to excite the senses, and endless ways to have fun, along with a good deal of the personal power we craved, why doesn't it work out like the fairytale we envisioned it to be?

And why do so many of us strive so hard to continue to exponentialize what we have *even after* we have reached the End Game?

As a great spiritual master once said, "There are only two ways of growing: growing old, which leads to death, and growing up, which leads to God."

Constantly spending money on ourselves may not have the intended result if we are merely growing old and not growing up in the process. The fulfillment we sought will usually continue to escape us.

As far as the deeper journey is concerned, we usually think first about being generous—giving to our family and friends instead of just to ourselves. But being generous to them with our money (especially as a substitute for our time and attention), or leaving a fortune to them in our estate at the time of our passing, may not have the intended result.

Heirs often become dependent upon your fiscal goodwill, thereby not developing their own will, their own sense of independence, or a feeling of self-worth. There have been plenty of examples of this backfiring of intended goodwill that I am sure you are all too aware of—there's no need for me to embellish those sad stories about the "lost" children of multigenerational families, some of which are now legendary.

More importantly, all of this hypothetical giving to family and friends and charities *still does not get to the heart of the question*: Whom do you serve?

The question is not "Whom do you wish to serve?" but rather "Whom are you serving?"—like it or not!

So here is the final story I will leave you with.

In the book *He*, by Robert Johnson (Harper & Row, 1989), a book about the male part of the human psyche, the knighted heroic fool, Parsifal (or Percival) is in search of the meaning of life, which only the fabled Holy Grail can supply the answer to.

The Grail plays a different role in different legends, but in most versions the hero must prove himself worthy to be in the Grail's presence. Parsifal knows the Grail is filled with many supernatural powers. Whomever it serves is automatically filled with health, riches, and all the other wonderful gifts in life we all wish for, material, psychological, and otherwise.

Parsifal's lack of wisdom prevents him from fulfilling his destiny when he first encounters the Grail. He is so in awe of what he is seeing, including the wounded Fisher King and the King's castle, that he fails to ask the question "Whom does the Grail serve?" The next morning, because he did not ask this crucial question, which all seekers must ultimately ask, he is sent away, and the castle disappears behind him.

Now, after years of searching and a thousand personal battles fought, he once again somehow arrives at the Grail castle's magical gate. He vows not to fail a second time.

Upon entering the Great Hall, he sees, as he did the first time, the wounded Fisher King. He's shocked and wonders to himself: If the Holy Grail is so powerful, why is this Fisher King still wounded and lying ill, and why is his entire kingdom darkened and the women unable to bear children? Why are the fields of such an opulent land barren? Why does no one show any joy in a land potentially so richly bestowed?

Finally he meets up with the Holy Grail itself, and Parsifal quickly remembers to ask, "*Whom does the Grail serve?*"

The Grail answers that it serves the Grail King.

Parsifal is a bit confused by this. It did not say it served the Fisher King or his countrymen. It would not serve Parsifal even though he had succeeded in finding it, or Parsifal's King Arthur. The Grail serves another king, a king that exists only in the center of the castle (metaphorically, the center of us). The Grail serves only the inner life.

Here is the key to the story: Once the question "Whom does the Grail serve?" is asked by Parsifal, the Fisher King's wound is immediately healed, the land is transformed with births, gardens bloom, and celebrations abound.

This is an amazing ending to the story of Parsifal, because the very question itself allowed the inner transformation to begin! It allowed the healing of the kingdom and the Fisher King to take place from the inside out.

The Game Beyond the End Game's true purpose is revealed in this story: If we do not endeavor to find the answers to our own life's questions, the wounds of this world may remain with us far too long. Our failures may poison us instead of making us stronger, and we may never be able to shake the terrible burdens of money, and all the meaningless goals that this modern culture lays before us.

The king shall be a slave. The wounds will not heal. And we will be defeated, all the while clothed in riches.

The answer to "Whom do we serve?" is: We serve our inner life, or we die a beggar.

I know this is an odd answer to questions that originate from "How do I safely invest my money?" But what I am suggesting is that without approaching a question like "How do I invest my money?" in a deep and conscious way, the answers you come up with may be filled with more failures, trapdoors, and mazes than answers.

The most pragmatic and successful answers ultimately have to come from how you want to live your life and how you want to play the game, not just which stock or hedge fund or mutual fund or piece of real estate to buy or sell.

Focusing on the question "Whom do you serve?" will hopefully prevent us from working with people or organizations we do not—and should not—ultimately want to be involved with.

It can guide us to a different set of personal relationships, including perhaps who we marry and who our children become.

It can prevent us from becoming addicted to the investment casino, a casino that has too many ways to beat us at a game that ultimately is not ours.

It can prevent us from buying the kinds of material things that in the end simply put a tighter choke hold around our precious free time and energy.

It can allow us to make choices that connect us to, rather than disconnect us from, the true riches in life.

In the end, by avoiding the many traps that inevitably accompany wealth and power, it may allow us to leave our children and spouse, and all of our heirs, so much more than all the land or money they may inherit from us.

It could leave them with the greatest legacy anyone, or any estate, could possibly leave: the map to the Grail Castle, and the right questions to ask once they have arrived.

Appendix

Specific Due Diligence Notes and Fund of Funds Questionnaire

Note 1: The following is not meant to be a full or comprehensive list of questions, nor can responsibility be taken for the timing, reliability, or effectiveness of the questions or the answers given. This is a suggested outline to allow for the beginning of an effective, trustworthy relationship between an investor and a manager or firm.

Note 2: Receiving the answers to these questions is *not* due diligence. The questions are inquiries that will generate answers from the manager or firm. *Checking the validity of their answers* is due diligence.

Investing in funds of funds is what I strongly suggest for qualified individual investors when moving assets into the hedge fund world. Funds of funds offer automatic diversification. It is also far easier to perform due diligence with respect to a fund of funds and ensure it is not fraudulent than to complete the same process for a single fund, or a group of single funds. This is because funds of funds are only compiling information from underlying managers, not trading. If the accountant and auditor are receiving the performances of the underlying managers independently from the fund of funds firm, you would then rely on the accountant's estimates, K-1s, and the annual audit, to prevent dishonesty at the fund level. This compares with the audits or K-1s of single managers who are each making hundreds of trades a year, potentially with more than one prime broker or trading account within their limited partnership.

You are welcome to use the following questionnaire. However, make sure you assess the results only after your follow-up calls to the fund's accountant and auditor. Doing so should be a solid first step in the investment process.

Also please review the "Using Etiquette, Receiving Respect: The General Partner/Limited Partner Relationship" section in Chapter 8 before contacting the fund.

FUND OF FUNDS QUESTIONNAIRE

Ask the general partner (GP) of the fund of funds to fill out this questionnaire. (The GP and staff should be familiar with this process and should be more than willing to get answers to all your questions within a few weeks.) Get their answers in writing for your files. Do not accept verbal responses.

Do not send this questionnaire with the boldface comments in parentheses included. They are just for you!

What are the fund's present unleveraged assets under management (AUM) (onshore/offshore separately)?

(A fund with $50 million or less is small, while $500 million is a very large fund. Between $100 million and $200 million is typical.)

If the fund uses leverage, how much leverage is deployed, and what are the notional (leveraged) assets under management?

Do you try to make economic, sector, or market calls to give the fund an edge?

How many managers do you have in the fund, and what are the highest-percentage allocations to the top managers?

(Ten managers or less is concentrated. Fifty managers or more could be too diversified.)

What is the highest allocation percentage you would ever give a single manager?

(Twenty percent is large. More than that is extreme.)

What percentage of the fund's underlying assets is invested in separately managed accounts in the fund's name—versus investing the fund in other limited partnerships?

Please describe *your* due diligence process for potential and current underlying managers.

(This is critical. Ask lots of follow-up questions like: Do they have on-site visits with all the managers? If so, how often?)

Are you invested in any small-cap or micro-cap funds, Regulation D funds, or private investments in public equity (PIPE) funds? If so, please tell us more about them.

(This needs to be explored with some caution because of the illiquid nature of these kinds of investments.)

What are the fund's performance goals annually?

Do you have underlying fund insurance covering your underlying managers against fraud or theft? Do you have errors and omissions (E&O) insurance? It is charged to the partnership or do you pay for it?

(The fund does usually pay for this. Most funds of funds do not have insurance coverage that would benefit the limited partner—you.)

Fees and expenses: What are the fund's lockups, entry points, withdrawal points, high-water mark, and hurdle rate?

Fund gate: Does the fund have a gate? If so, please explain the process once the gate is triggered.

(This means you may only be able to withdraw your money incrementally.)

Are you willing to supply e-mailed weekly or bimonthly performance estimates?

(Very rough intramonth estimates are not uncommon.)

How many partners do you have in the fund(s) (onshore/offshore separately)?

How many other funds, separately managed accounts, or other types of strategies are the principals of the firm managing?

Please state the firm's total assets under management.

Is the fund part of one or more affiliated firms? If so, name them, and what are the affiliated firm(s)' assets under management? Please provide contact names and numbers.

Transparency: What level of transparency regarding the fund portfolio are you willing to provide, and at what frequency? A pie chart with the underlying fund's strategies and the percentage of assets in each underlying fund would be sufficient.

What is the allowable frequency of access to your general partner/manager by phone and/or e-mail?

Will you sign a side letter that allows us to receive withdrawn (or 90 percent of any redeemed) monies within 10 business days of the withdrawal date unless there is an extreme liquidity event?

(Potentially long withholding periods of your assets after the withdrawal date need to be considered and understood before investing.)

If you are using leverage, please describe whether it is an option, or what other form it is in.

(Be extremely careful about leverage being used on funds that have volatile performances.)

Which bank(s) provide(s) the leverage for the fund?

Real-time Performance: Please provide the monthly returns *net of all fees* since inception in a one-page summary document for each of your funds and products past and present. Do not include pro forma (back-tested) numbers.

Who is your:

Accountant, administrator, and/or bank custodian? Please provide all relevant details regarding the firms plus contact persons and phone numbers.

Auditor: From whom does the auditor get the monthly statements and relevant prices of the portfolio in order to proceed with the annual audit? Please provide all relevant details of the auditing firm plus a contact person and phone number.

Internal authorized signatories: How many signatures are needed and from whom in order for assets to be withdrawn from the fund by the fund principals?

External authorized signatories: How many signatures are needed and from whom in order for assets to be wired from the fund to other funds or partners?

(Check all of the above for accuracy. Call the accountant and/or administrator if there is one, and the auditor directly, to ensure they are independent of the fund of funds and are happy with their relationship.)

(Verify that they get the performances of the underlying managers independently from the fund itself. You do not want the fund supplying the performance numbers to the accountant since theoretically the fund could then fabricate numbers. Verify that the accountant also gets the fund's bank statements and notices of wires in and out of the fund directly from the bank(s), not from the fund.)

(You should receive your account information quarterly or monthly—usually with a delay of four to six weeks—directly from the fund administrator or accountant. The accounting firm or administrator must be independent of the fund of funds firm itself. *If the fund is generating in-house statements, or no statements, don't invest.*)

(K-1s may be delayed *well past* the April 15 tax deadline, sometimes by months. This is not uncommon and you should expect to file for an extension.)

HISTORY AND STRUCTURE OF THE ORGANIZATION

In what year was the firm and/or fund founded?

Are there any major seed investors? Name the top four investors in terms of percentage of assets they have in the fund.

Describe any changes in the structure of the firm or fund over the past five years. For example, has the fund or firm been bought by another entity? Has the fund changed strategies since its inception?

Are there any such changes presently contemplated or being discussed internally?

Briefly outline succession plans if/when the main principal retires.

Are there any plans to start other funds or limited partnerships with the same or differing styles? Would any principal be involved in that venture not presently in the firm?

Have any funds, accounts, or strategies been discontinued or merged in the past five years? If so, what were the circumstances?

Has the Securities and Exchange Commission (SEC) or any other regulator ever audited your firm? If yes, please describe the reason for the audit and the results.

Please disclose any litigation, complaints, arbitration, or other disputes involving your fund, your affiliated firm, your manager, the principals, and/or your employees in the past seven years, or pending at present. Include the nature of the action and the outcome, if resolved.

What is the division of power/responsibilities among the principals?

Describe any family relationships within the business structure.

What are the total number of employees and their functions?

Who is the fund attorney? Please supply contact person and phone number.

What has been the most serious issue the fund attorney has had to deal with since inception?

Is the fund attorney also the personal or business-related attorney for the individual principals in the fund?

Manager profile: Please answer for each relevant individual:

What are the city, state, and country of all of your current residence(s) and personal office(s) other than the fund's primary office?

Please provide general partner(s)' and chief investment officer's two places of employment directly previous to this one.

Please provide the names and phone numbers of the last two past employers for references.

What colleges/universities, including graduate programs, did you graduate from? List degrees.

How often do you communicate with the underlying funds and traders?

Have any of the principals ever filed for bankruptcy either personally or within a business format?

Have any of the principals ever had or is there any pending legal, SEC, or other complaints or lawsuits filed against them personally, or against any of their previous employers or co-partner/owners? If yes, please explain.

Manager and management team: Please answer for each relevant individual:

Age:

Marital status:

How long have you lived in your current residence?

Have you ever had any life-threatening illnesses or injuries? What, if any, effect do they have at present on your health and work?

Have you ever been under treatment, in counseling, or arrested for drinking or drugs, or any felony?

PRESENT INVESTORS

What percentage of liquid net worth of the principals is invested in the fund?

What is the approximate percentage of other partner and/or client assets?

> Other fund employees
>
> Individuals
>
> Corporate
>
> Institutional investment company/fund
>
> Pension/IRA
>
> Funds of funds
>
> Endowments/foundations

Please provide the names of a few current investors as references. Please include those who may be institutional and have done their own professional due diligence.

FUND REPORTING

What fully independent source can verify the performance of the fund? Please include contact information.

(The performance needs to be verified with that source.)

From whom does this independent administrator get the underlying performance data (direct feed from the underlying manager, or other)? If other, please describe.

How long have you known and worked with your administrator and accountant?

Did you or any affiliate of yours have a previous relationship with your administrator or accountant?

Who was your previous administrator or accountant, if any? Contact and phone:

Is the auditor fully independent from the firm and you?

(The answer to this must be yes or you should not invest.)

How does the auditor track the fund's assets during an audit? Just by following the cash, or by reconciling each manager's independent monthly estimates?

(The auditor needs to be contacted. The above answers need to be verified. Only following the cash is not acceptable. The auditor must get independent information from each of the underlying managers.)

Were there any problems with any previous audits? If so, please describe.

Were there any problems with audits at firms where you were previously employed?

Who is the custodian of the assets?

Contact person and phone number:

OPERATIONAL ISSUES

What happens in case of death or injury to the fund's primary portfolio manager?

REAL-TIME ISSUES

Explain why your largest drawdown happened.

At what point would you consider closing the fund to new money? Why?

STRATEGY

Briefly describe the following (or supply prewritten materials):

The fund's strategy and objectives.

Specific monthly and annual risk and return objectives for the fund.

How does the fund differentiate itself from others in its strategy class? What is your edge?

What benchmark do you feel is most appropriate to measure performance against?

In which type of markets does your strategy perform best/worst?

Will you commit to informing us if your strategy is about to change, or if any change is being contemplated?

If a strategy is about to change, will you offer us an opportunity to fully redeem before this strategy takes effect?

What is the best percentage month and year you might imagine having within the parameters of your stated strategy?

What is the worst percentage month and year you might imagine having within the parameters of your stated strategy?

LEVERAGE

What are the average amount and the maximum amount of leverage used by the fund?

What percentage of the underlying managers uses leverage?

What is the maximum leverage used by any of your managers?

TAXES

Is the fund particularly advantageous or disadvantageous for either tax-exempt investors or tax-paying investors? Please supply us with past years' K-1s so we can assess the tax basis of the fund on an annualized basis.

(Most funds of funds generate approximately 100 percent short-term capital gains or ordinary income. Some funds can generate more than 100 percent short-term gains or ordinary income due to events such as the accumulation of unrealized losses. Avoid those funds. The tax will usually vary from year to year.)

Explain your tax assessment process both before and during your investment with an underlying manager.

K-1 TIMING

Could you please supply the approximate dates of previous years' K-1 deliveries to partners?

(It is typical that a fund of funds will provide K-1s long after the April 15 tax deadline due to the time necessary to collect the underlying fund K-1s. Extensions to your tax reporting are usually necessary.)

Signatures of the general partners are required here. If more than two, please sign as well.

_____   Date _____

_____   Date _____

Please include with this report your most recent audit and your current SEC Form ADV.

About the Author

Celebrated money manager and rock songwriter Gary Marks has achieved great success in two distinctly different careers.

Gary is highly regarded in the securities industry for his innovative work as the CEO and sole owner of Sky Bell Asset Management, an alternative investment firm with affiliated offices in Florida, New York, and Hawaii. He founded Sky Bell in July of 1999 and the firm now manages nearly $300 million.

Sky Bell creates and manages specifically targeted hedged funds of funds for qualified investors. Sky Bell is also known in the financial industry for its unique ability to form affiliations with firms normally considered to be competitors in the field.

Simultaneously, Gary still actively writes songs, sings, plays piano and guitar, and records CDs of his original music. All of Gary's music can be found on iTunes.

In 1973, at the age of 23, Gary recorded and released *Gathering*, his first of 10 critically acclaimed recordings. *Gathering* was re-released internationally in 2007 by an independent European record label as a "rock-jazz classic." His 10th CD, *A Whisper Can Change the World*, was released early in 2007.

He finds the time for both careers by actively practicing the four strategies discussed in this book.

Please feel free to visit Gary's web site to listen to his music at www.GaryMarksMusic.com.

See his free music offer at the back of the book.

You are also invited to visit Gary's financial web site at www.RockingWallStreet.com.

Gary currently lives in Maui, Hawaii, with his wife and three young children.

Index

To learn more about Gary Marks and his music, please visit his web site:

www.GaryMarksMusic.com

As a special thank-you for purchasing *Rocking Wall Street*, Gary would like to offer you **two free songs** from his latest CD, "A Whisper Can Change the World."

On the home page just click on the "Rocking Wall Street" link and follow instructions to get your free digital downloads.

We also invite you to visit the Gary Marks financial web site:

www.RockingWallStreet.com